◆

life, you are a gash in need of stitching

mpT
MODERN POETRY IN TRANSLATION

The best of world poetry

No.3 2017
© *Modern Poetry in Translation* 2017 and contributors

ISSN (print) 0969-3572
ISSN (online) 2052-3017
ISBN (print) 978-1-910485-18-7

Editor: Sasha Dugdale
Managing Editor: Deborah de Kock
Development Manager: Sarah Hesketh
Web and Communications Manager: Ed Cottrell
Design by Jenny Flynn
Cover art by Nicola Samonov

Printed and bound in Great Britain by Charlesworth Press, Wakefield
For submissions and subscriptions please visit www.mptmagazine.com

Modern Poetry in Translation Limited. A Company Limited by Guarantee
Registered in England and Wales, Number 5881603
UK Registered Charity Number 1118223

Supported using public funding by
ARTS COUNCIL ENGLAND

We are grateful to the Case Foundation for their support for this issue. Poems in the issue will be published in *Words for War: New Poems from Ukraine* (forthcoming from Academic Studies Press, Boston) and these translations are funded by the National Endowment from the Humanities and Ukranian Research Institute, Harvard University.

NATIONAL ENDOWMENT FOR THE HUMANITIES

Academic Studies Press

MODERN POETRY IN TRANSLATION

War of the Beasts and the Animals

CONTENTS

Reviews

EDITORIAL

This, my last, issue of MPT features poems of conflict and protest
from Russia and Ukraine. The conflict in the Donbas region of
Ukraine is politically intricate, and at the same time it is diabolically
simple. In 2014 Russia covertly invaded an area of Ukraine with an
ethnically and linguistically Russian population after illegally
annexing the Crimea. A fierce war broke out, with daily casualties and
atrocities, and even now it smoulders on in the area. Propaganda and
false truths draw a veil over the war and its many casualties and
victims, and serve at the same time to heap grievance upon grievance;
to ensure that peace will remain provisional and uneasy.

A generation of Ukrainian poets has risen to the challenge with
war poems of exceptional honesty, integrity and courage. If you want
to know what it feels like to live through a European twenty-first
century war then you should start by reading this poetry, just as you
might well start with the poetry of the First World War. Poetry in
war has a heightened significance because, as Ilya Kaminsky writes,
it 'like a seismograph, registers the violating occurences' that everyday
forms of language are no longer able to measure. Poetry continues
to insist on the seismic tremors of Keats's 'felt truth'. Awkward,
uncomfortable and deeply individual, 'felt truth' resists the monolith
of propaganda and the easy generalisations of foreign policy and
journalism. It also resists the glamour of sacrifice and the glibness
of despair. As Serhiy Zhadan writes of a war victim: 'There will
come a time when some bastard will surely write heroic poems about
this. | There will come a time when some other bastard will say this
isn't worth writing about.' (p.128)

It's worth noting here that the number of Ukrainian poets includes
some Russian-speaking poets, as Ukraine is linguistically divided and
many of her citizens have two mother tongues. The front line is along
ethnic and linguistic lines of difference; however many Ukrainians
will say that until the protests in Kiev in 2013 the differences between

Culture is simply the lubrication needed to insert a people into a new war

The very first issue of *Modern Poetry in Translation* is now online at www.modernpoetryintranslation.com

East and West were at the level of jokes about ethnic stereotypes. The poetry by Russian authors here is equally unsettling because it lays bare a fractured and troubled post-Soviet landscape and a poetics which is born of anxiety and loneliness.

I have translated and included here Maria Stepanova's poem 'War of the Beasts and the Animals', because it is a direct commentary on the war in Ukraine: 'a civil war' as Stepanova has said, 'in the sense that all wars are civil wars', although of course it is also a civil war in the sense that both sides have a common tongue and a common Soviet and imperial history.

Stepanova explodes the martial culture and jingoism of post-Soviet Russia into a million constituent splinters and shows the complicity of culture in violence. Culture is simply the lubrication needed to insert a people into a new war: the erosion of real memory by mythmaking, the destruction of real humans in the fabrication of heroes. 'War of the Beasts and Animals' is a new modernist poem, political, angry and lyrical.

The poetry from this region has never been more necessary to us. It provides us with a true insight into modern war and its psychological effects, measured with the finest instruments: lyric poets. With its truth-saying powers it also alerts us to the danger of imperial reach and the glorification of nationalism and military might. There is much that prophetic Russian poets can tell us about our own future.

Sasha Dugdale

MURATHAN MUNGAN

Translated by Aron Aji and David Gramling

The poems included here come from Murathan Mungan's,
Kalbimin Dogusunda (My Heart's East), a collection of poems inspired
by and about the rich and difficult cultural geography of south-
east Turkey. Written throughout Murathan's writing career, the
poems pay homage to his multi-ethnic, Kurdish-Arab-Turkish
formation; at the same time, because of the range of themes and
the lush poetics that are in full display among these poems, the
collection also serves as a signature work, representing Mungan's
literary breadth and achievement beautifully. Drawn from eleven
discrete volumes, the poems invoke their original volumes, mapping
for us the aesthetics and thematic currents that permeate Mungan's
writing: tradition and individuality, religious dogma, ethnicity
vs. tribalism, politics of gender and sexuality, fractured memory,
alterity, among others.

Mungan is deeply attached to the plain, vernacular language,
which accommodates considerable lyricism because of its natural
musicality – due to vowel harmonies and inflections – and because
the line between the figurative and the literal is often unclear
(especially when compared with English), yielding vividly expressive
poetic imagery. Mungan's attention to the rich particularity of
human stories makes his lyricism all the more magnetic. A reserve
of private memories – ultimately enigmatic and inaccessible –
creates an irresistibly subjective core to his poetry. At the same
time, true to the Turkish lyric tradition and, really, all great lyrical
poetry, the personal is inseparable from the public or the political
in Mungan; *Kalbimin Dogusunda* is as much the memory of the
poet as it is the memory of the people and the scarred landscape
of south-east Turkey. It is fitting that it was the first collection of

poems to have been released in Kurdish translation by a major
Turkish publishing house (Metis). Titled *Li Rojhilatê Dilê Min*, the
volume was originally published in 1996, then as an expanded
bilingual edition in 2012.

Blood Creatures

yellow blooms in autumn's ledger
birds' feet, carriers of migrant sensation
lament, every man's forest
cuts a whistle through the tree bark
nothing will hold us back any longer
not even the forest blazes inside us
we move – the clouds, heavy daggers down our backs
we move – bodies hollowed as our tree hollows
our adventures are bloody trails
we are blood countries
as if the unerring Sirat would let us through
no: hell after hell after hell
all hells for us
on our feet a false god's wooden soles
so, too, our petitions remain unread
for we are blood countries
our beauty gone lost in all this blood
birds claw at our lips
across an autumn, our footprints
tarnish all the mirrors with their viral rage
this is all there is: we must not die

Twenty Thousand Stars

twenty thousand stars fell to earth
twenty thousand leaves
which history will recall – how? what part?

the killed, who were they? the killers, who?
the survivors, how misled are they about surviving?
history's hearing, mortal examination
impassive ploughfields gone to graves

stars die in the east
as light, they spin back to earth
the great republic of the dead
one day the borders will breach
tribes, customs, nations
states, flags, heroes
the dead, too, will breach one day
we will be naked, naked on the morning of every man's world
our bodies, once dead as stars, will burst into leaf
those who call the same earth homeland in two separate tongues
will meet beneath that same earth

the east's lost sky, on its graveclothes
twenty thousand stars flare among the light years
when we remember

We Did Not Forget

wounded holy days come and gone
seasons, too, with all their meaning
dregs settled deep in the heart
come and gone in due time
come and gone the cities and the dead
we did not forget

from the black earth to the pole star
everywhere, everything
seemed possible
we were as joyful as Nazım
as lovestruck as Aragon
as wounded as Lorca
we did not forget

over there, a ravaged geography
over there, offset-print newspapers
over there, 835 lines written over again
and cities that will not give in to despair

we laid the sky's dark shroud over
your dead – corpses riddled with stars –
the unnamed, the bodies known
only by place names we forgot
yet we forgot none of you

That was the age of war and trade
we used the same markets
shed the same blood, armed
with the same weapons
called on hearts unmoved by love or bullets
we passed through ambushes, plundered gardens
a history in ruin
we saw men born of combat
swift to sleep, rifles cradled in their arms
quick to sulk like children
and to cheer like the poppies
legions passing through
history's longest night

same blood in those markets
same money exchanged in dark trading posts
same bloodied history time upon time
only we survived – too caught up in being alive
standing so near death – just us
and the chorus of ten thousands
intifada intifada intifada

we had beauty, twofold
the one the bullets took away
the other, offset-print photographs
thirty-three bullets shot into every one of us
on those eastern days and nights
thirty-three stars – as remote as the arctic
as near as home's hearth – still dispatch their light to us

flints in my pocket
a couple of cloves
silk for the road, yeast for insomnia
for your heart I bring words
naked and severe, like a black oath
in this country of lost centuries
death even comes after the children
I won't stay with you in the mountains
just came to bring water for your flasks
in the ditches this age cannot cross
I come and go and come
between mirage and truth
as joyful as Nazım
as lovestruck as Aragon
as wounded as Lorca

lightflash at the trailheads
where legends proliferate
ages hide in an instant
fire's Avestan tongue
plants, herbs, roots
pomegranate's colour
branded tongues
counting the tens of thousands' return
on the east's new ledger
from the black earth to the pole star
everywhere, everything
in a dark ambush

o great mesopotamia
among the first children
of writing, of the wheel, of history
o night of two thousand years
                    turn around, look:
my brothers and sisters are dying
in my heart's east

Dawn and Shahmaran

over and over I've been lynched
every piece of my flesh, like Shahmaran
ask any mountain, it's its custom:
the serpent lies beneath the stone

o drowning one! your eyes track me like a mountain range
enfold the dark history in your dark love
this caravan will not go far under the usurper's yoke
victory, though late, will come to the losers
the day will break one day
one day the war stories will return, restored
will begin again, like Shahmaran – she who shed her scales –
our songs will billow in the banner of our voices
mountains will brim over into the main squares
of cities shattered at the sound of a whistle long in wait
a mid-east tale, tangled in its own prayer beads*
prey to oblivion, like the images of Shahmaran, relics of old walls

the histories of fear, tyranny and love, retold
in the pictures of a defiant people
will illuminate the sky alongside the histories of rebirth
passing through our lives
that is, through the exile of labour and love
through battles lost in shallow trenches
through earthquakes on feudal fault lines
her shattered body made whole
etched across a new dawn

* as best as history can remember

KAMALABOOSHANI THIRUNAVUKKARASU

Translated by Malliha Sinniah, Thirunavukkarasu and
Vidyan Ravinthiran

Kamalabooshani Thirunavukkarasu was born almost a hundred
years ago, and lost her mother when young. She was nurtured in her
reading by a teacher we know only as Miss Atkins – an Englishwoman
who remained in Sri Lanka after it gained independence – and who
encouraged this Tamil girl, from Batticaloa on the east coast, to read
and read.

My grandmother passed this passion down the generations. She
was deeply interested in poetry, in both English and Tamil, and my
father describes the starlit nights when he, his mother and his sister
would lie on mats of coconut leaf, on the soft sand of their rear yard,
and look up at the sky – and Kamala would come up with the first
two lines of a poem. This was a challenge to her children, who would
compete with each other to continue it.

After the death of her husband, Kamala balanced, somehow, the
bringing up of five children with the demanding role of Principal
at a girls' college. She was a noted orator, both on the stage and the
radio; a prolific author of prose and verse; a writer of plays; and a
guardian of dispossessed young women without a dowry.

Of her written work, two exercise books of Tamil verse have
survived, containing these poems, among others.

Squirrel

The shadow of the gold flower
isn't enough for you, is it? Nor
the petals of the neem that glow like snow.
Still you aren't tired. You go on

through the branches of the punnai,
grazed by the edge of each coconut leaf.
What's bothering you? Too many cashews;
or that orange, thorny branch?

Hairy, pink florets allure. And you sniff
along the rooftop tiles and dream
of a proffered handful of nuts. Oh, squirrel:
does that crow scare you? You could rest

in a fanlike leaf, or the flower-face
of the pooravasu. There are shadows
upon shadows, of the tamarind
leaf; tall palms, with their coconuts.

And here are the juicy mangoes.
Can you enjoy it all? Is there time?
Away from flowers, fruits, leaves
you sleep in your burrow in the dead trunk.

None of these gave you the love
you were after. So be content
with what you have in hand.
The sweetest joy is a pellucid mind.

Otherwise, to search elsewhere,
travelling far from your own
life that comes and goes: will that,
my squirrel, yield true pleasure?

No Milk

Hastening through her chores of a morning
she sweeps,
dusts,
draws with rice flour
the geometric
kolam on the floor;

washing, and cleaning;

with her mathu
the butter is churned.
She piles the firewood high
and coaxes a flame
with little inserted twigs.
The red fire leaps.

Sticking the kettle on

she goes for milk. But,
walking to the cow
with her brass sembu in hand

buffed to a gold shine,
she turns to a statue.
Broken loose

from his rope

the calf,
wheedling and demanding,
nuzzling close,
his tail a prong,
has taken all his mother's milk
for himself!

She begins to cry.

Thinking of her baby
son, and how
she kissed his soft hand
and held him tightly.
Love upwelled in her.
He sucked and sucked,

wanting more from her.

She remembers
moving her breast
to look at his face;
tickling him, as she wiped away
the spilled milk.
Licking its calf, the cow knew joy!

Losing her son, the mother went empty and dry.

Now she hears a voice: *amma*.
The sembu slips from her hand.
The sound
of the temple bells
sweeps her mind
clean. The morning tea is black.

'Why?' asks her husband. 'No milk,' she says.

The Kallady Bridge

takes its blue from the sky above,
and spans the brown lagoon
in which the famous singing fish
goes for night swims with the moon.

– The moon, reflected in the flow,
as cars and cycles trundle down
the famous bridge, across whose length
children crowd, and run.

– The Kallady bridge has tales to tell.
Here's a girl with shining hair
her beau strolls towards the town;
love-birds, who self-compare

with those of the silver screen.
When amma and appa
urge her marriage to another
she dreams, still, of her boy-lover.

Her schoolgirl friends tell little lies
to cover for her changing moods;
he tries to lose himself in drink
and goes for long walks in the woods.

How could he, how could she,
destroy a mother's peace of mind;
a husband's, and a father's, honour?
Thus the lovers grieved and pined.

'To walk beneath the panthal
covered with its white wedding cloth;
will this stir love for the stranger
to whom I am betrothed?

Will a hasty ceremony
give me my happiness back,
once he fastens the shining thali
around my reluctant neck?'

She lost weight, and shunned her jewels.
It broke her husband's heart.
She seemed to rot like an unplucked fruit.
'Is there love in her?' he asked.

'Even a backward village-girl
would show more love
to her chosen groom. For what
is fame and wealth without love?'

He feels wronged, and shouts at her;
to heal the ravaged moment,
she yields herself to him;
a defeated opponent.

Now, at last, he's happy!
This, he thinks, is true marriage!
But in the middle of the night
she creeps to the fateful bridge.

Sobbing, helpless, suddenly
everything seems clear.
What she must do, where she must go,
is written on the water of each tear.

There is nothing else for it.
Her husband is infatuated
with a phantom. And her lover
now spends his days intoxicated.

Mark this: she wasn't the first,
and won't be the last, to leap
from the bridge into the lagoon
while all the town is fast asleep.

But fate was having none of it.
A brave fisherman saw it all.
He jumped into the water
and rescued her; and thus she fell

into a state of death-in-life. Now
her passions are housebound.
See her there, standing at her doorstep,
awaiting her lawful husband.

CHRISTOPHE TARKOS

translated by Beverley Bie Brahic

'Ideas are not my strong point,' the French poet Francis Ponge protested, perhaps too much, in *My Creative Method* (1947). Ponge, who claimed that what he *was* good at was description-definitions of *things* (rain, pebbles), is a poet with whom Christophe Tarkos (see 'It is snowing') has affinities; one might also evoke the Perec of *Tentative d'épuisement d'un lieu* or the Beckett of *Texts for Nothing*.

Tarkos was born near Marseille in 1963 and died, at the age of 40, of a brain tumour, in 2004. In the last 10 years of his life, in and out of hospital, he created furiously, publishing over 20 books and giving dozens of performance / improvisations (some of them viewable online). He pleaded for the text's materiality, inventing the term 'pâte-mot / patmo' or 'word-dough' for his approach to language's slipperiness; in Tarkos text and sound together become a way to think, to think about thinking, and, ultimately, to act: 'The text is not a means to something else, it is itself something. The truth of the text is the palpable material existence of the text,' he said in a 1996 interview.

Tarkos's words and syntax are plain; like litanies or rituals, they repeat obsessively, with infinitesimal variations. Nonetheless, and even when it appears to seek emotional flatness, his language feels lyrical, its sounds and rhythms musical. Sliding across the surfaces of words, poems may, for instance, enumerate all the objects in a bathroom, projecting, in the manner of, say, a Chardin still life with its casually-dropped knife or half-empty glass, a portrait of the absent, but surely close-by, human being. Such poems seem to need to pin down and contain a world in which everything is destined to disappear, including, of course – and in Tarkos's case, especially poignantly – the author. They tunnel into the limits of our knowledge about the 'perfect fortress' (Calvino, 'The Count of

Monte Cristo') 'from which one cannot escape.' In a 1998 interview, Tarkos said his poems were filled with nostalgia: '...the nostalgia of being able to come back but one can't come back. One is caught in the flow of speech, in time's ongoingness.'

Anachronisme (2001), from which these texts are taken, was the last book Tarkos published before his death.

It is snowing. Small flakes spin in all directions, I see them rise, in the wind the flakes spin, they are light, they go crosswise and they go up, it is snowing, the flakes don't act like the straight stripes of rain, they are light, they blow wherever the wind blows them, or the movements of the air, in every direction, they smack my cheek, sting my eyes, are small and hard, it is snowing small flakes, I don't know if the snow will stay, if in a second the countryside will be covered in snowy white, it seems to be staying, the road is already all white and so is the park, the horizontal grass of the park and the branches of bushes and trees have been whitened, are already covered with a thin sheet of snow, from the flakes turning in every direction, that are small in size, that roll down the roads, skim the ground and the leaves, that stick in nooks and crannies, at the base of telephone poles, in the corners of walls, it seems to be staying, it will stay, it is nightfall, the white snow on the roads is lit up, the sky seems endless, filled with snow, seems to have infinite reserves of snow in the sky, it sifts down, touch by touch, small flake by small flake, small ball by small ball, that do not stay then stay, that want to collect, to hold onto each other, to cling, the road is already white, the flakes stick to the wool of my coat and my hat, I whiten, I shift my hat so the snow stops hitting my face, the wind is strong, night is falling, the flakes swirl in the light from the lamps at the corner of the street, the flakes are tiny, they whiten the whole park, how many flakes are falling so as to cover an entire park, tap-tapping the park with thousands of tiny touches. The sky has changed into snow, the sky pours out snow without seeming to be able to stop. The snow seems to be staying on the ground.

◆

Five widows. My five previous mistresses were five widows. This doesn't make sense. I don't try to make sense of it, I didn't realize this, then one day, I thought she's a widow, oh, this one too, the next one is a widow, then the third, then the fourth, then the fifth, my five previous mistresses were widows, women who were married then lost their husbands in an accident, brutally, not a natural death, a sudden blow of fate, a kidnapping, these five widows were young since they were my mistresses, there isn't any age for becoming a widow, with them I had a special sexual relation, some of them very young and already widowed, widows like virgins, they are brand new, how could they know, they didn't wear black, the mourning period was over, it was time to seek life again, make up for lost time, the memory of the dead husband must have been present, must have drifted about, I don't know, I have no way of knowing, all I know is that five widows made up this series of five mistresses, that there is no meaning to this, I can't use this as a basis for any mode of behaviour, fucking the first time I didn't know they were widows, I wasn't aware of this succession of just widows, it only strikes me today, today I see that my mistresses were widows, that this makes a series of five widows in my bed, five virgins, five widows, it is a coincidence, I haven't found any meaning.

◆

A towel, a bathrobe, a bathmat, a wastebasket, a horsehair mitt, perfume, a tooth glass, a soap dish, a cake of soap, toothbrushes, toothpaste, ether, a compress, a hair dryer, shears, bath salts from the dead sea, files, a rack, a facecloth, shampoo, a headband, tweezers, a barrette, a hairbrush, a grater, a shower cap, sanitary napkins, panty liners, tampons, makeup remover, sunscreen, a piece of string, a pair of glasses, a pen, a pencil, a screwdriver, scissors, a roll of scotch tape, sterculia gum, a radiator, a comb, a thermometer, a tablet of detergent, a sheet, a hairband, a depilator, cotton makeup remover pads, absorbent cotton, Q-tips, a curling iron, a bottle of efferalgan, a bathtub, a sink, a brush, some tissues, some shells.

◆

Names are haunting, they haunt me. They are used, they don't
become part of any generality, they don't serve a cause, they don't
want to submit to any simple, general, common rule, they don't want
to be broken down and grow longer and more flexible and change and
turn around and act in such a way as to serve on different and varied
occasions. I must file away all these names that haunt me. I don't
know what they are good for, I use them, they pop up instinctively,
they come from the depths where they don't sleep, where they
continue to move, to shift and to try to join up with the common,
usable terms, into sentences, parts of sentences, they don't want to
stay on their own without attachments, I must attach them so they
stop coming along on their own, slipping into the sentences right in
the middle of the sentences I am uttering, mixed up with normal
words, slotting right in, within the normal words as if they rise from
the same depths, I can't make a sentence without these undeclined
noun-names slipping, without warning, into the flow of the words,
as if they had the right to come into my mouth, like all the other
words which do have the right because they are common words, the
words that belong to everyone, words that expose themselves, that
don't exist, that change, that are declined. I don't want to write these
names down where all the words that don't exist are written down,
I don't want them to have a different sort of potency, a calming effect,
a certitude, as if everything I said served only to make the names
stick out.

◆

I know the names of sewing things, of couturiers, of bakers, of pastry chefs, of brands of groceries, of actors, of musicians, of doctors, of composers, of conductors, of theatres, of plays, of operas, of singers, of bands, of roads, of mountains, of royal families, of industrialists, of bankers, of banks, of Lolita Lempicka, of comedians, of soccer players, of athletes, of public works enterprises, of paper makers, of chalk makers, of shoemakers, of garden centres, of charitable organizations, of religions, of the great Russian families, of travel agencies, of trucking companies, of shipping companies, of government officials, of supermarket chains, of restaurants and cafés, of Marseille's neighbourhoods, of the inhabitants of La Ronze, of newspapers, of soft drinks, of cookies, of big hotels, of cousins, of villages, of cities, of highways, of gas stations, of cigarettes, of alcoholic beverages, of drinks served in cafés, of painters, of countries, of cheeses, of guns, of rivers, of mineral waters, of drugs, of the departments of France, of the beaches in Camargue, of cosmetics, of creams, of lipsticks, of shampoos, of dancers, of choreographers, of automobiles.

◆

TINA STROHEKER

Translated by Steph Morris

Selected from Tina Stroheker's prose poem sequence *Luftpost für eine Stelzengängerin. Notate vom Lieben* (Airmail for a Woman on Stilts – Notes from Love), the poems here describe a relationship between two women, of a certain age, and while love is in some senses universal, often this fact matters. The women's movement, pride marches (on stilts, hence the title), women's bars, prejudice, activism and rainbow accessories are all part of the texture of the affair, along with the ways you might create and assert an image you have determined for yourself; wear what you want and be what you want. But it's also about the usual nerves, courage, joys and fears involved in succumbing to love. And chocolate.

Tina Stroheker has also written 'travel poetry' or 'poetry of place', mainly about Poland, including a collection about the city of Lodz. Her Polish translator, from that city, told me she'd seen it again for the first time reading Tina's book, thanks to the detail and focus of the observations. I met them at the translators' centre in Straelen, Germany, where they were working on a Polish translation of this collection in which, again, we see affairs of the heart as if for the first time.

All these poems are published in the original German in *Luftpost für eine Stelzengängerin. Notate vom Lieben* (Tübingen: Klöpfer und Meyer, 2013).

The chocolate tastes bitter. The chocolate tastes sweet. You passed it over the table, a snack for my return journey. I have to leave again. And I've just had a taste of it, in the café. Your white shirt falls open at the chest; my mouth is suddenly dry. You've dressed up! And I have to leave again. Let's stay here a moment. We're waiting for the bill anyway. I have to leave. I want to come back here.

◆

I was at the rendezvous too early, as ever. And I really wanted to arrive after you: our first date. From the dim hallway of a block I peeped out at the street, holding a throwaway camera, spur-of-the-moment purchase. I saw you approach, ride past, brake at the café, park your bike, lock it, and enter. I turned back again and took a photo of my waiting place: shadows, bins with red lids, a noticeboard for the tenants, letter boxes, daylight beyond. And then I stepped out, into that light.

◆

Soldiers, prisoners, men on oil rigs, cling to their photos. And I have them pinned to the wall in my room. From there they wave to me as I open the window. Nan Goldin on her bed with Siobhan, Lotte Laserstein and her model Traute, Susan Sontag sitting on a table by a window, arm resting on a pile of books, the young Pat Highsmith, naked. I take deep breaths. Instead of working, I look over at the photos. Oil rig glances. I have to slow my breathing. One photo, not hanging on the wall, keeps pushing in front: you, stepping out of your shower, alone with your thoughts, an everyday epiphany. Breathe slowly, nice and slow. Something in me is trying to split away. My heart is a fruit about to fall, soft and defenceless, for all to see.

♦

My first name fits in yours. Could slip into it. Penetrate it. Some thoughts come from nowhere, but are hard to shake off. Keys on my laptop, soft tapping in my ears as I give them their exercise. And with the laptop's Morse I recall the dream sequence where I gave you two stuffed animals, one fitting in the other's belly. Toys, without instructions.

◆

Wunderbar, Stuttgart / *Ačko*, Brno / *Begine*, Berlin / *Bei Carla*, Munich / *Belladonna*, Konstanz / *Club Scena*, Wrocław / *Diva*, Olomouc / *Frauencafé*, Vienna / *Hanseatin*, Hamburg / *Home*, Ulm / *Karotte*, Munich / *King's Club*, Stuttgart / *La Leander*, Potsdam / *Laura's*, Stuttgart / *Orlando*, Bochum / *Rainbow Lounge*, Minden / *Rosa Villa*, Vienna / *Rosalinde*, Leipzig / *Sappho*, Dresden / *Sarah*, Stuttgart / *UnscheinBar*, Potsdam / *Zentrum Weissenburg*, Stuttgart / *Zum Alten Fritz*, Ulm: showgrounds, stages, training grounds, crime scenes, tearful scenes, meeting points (thank you!). One day, at one of them: you. Wunderbar.

◆

The chocolate tastes sweet. The chocolate tastes bitter. I bought it in the village shop and bit straight into it. I badly needed something sweet. Then I walked to the Rhine, sunscreen and towel in my rucksack. Swimming, I turned back into a seal, snorting and writhing in the water. The air was clear, only over Reichenau evening mist. I was a cheerful seal, didn't want to get out of the water and back on my two legs. But I was getting chilly and turned myself back into a woman, alone on a riverbank, eating the rest of a chocolate bar, packing up her things, and leaving.

◆

YANNIS RITSOS

Translated by David Harsent

Romiosini – literally 'Greekness' – is more an idea than a definition, and an idea that is notoriously difficult to explain. It looks back to having been part of the Roman Empire, more specifically to Byzantium, but doesn't fix or delineate nationality or even identity. Rather, it describes an emotional response to being Greek, though even to talk of description is to suggest a coherence that the term avoids. No two Greeks, it is said, would give the same definition of *romiosini*. It is felt. It is heart not head, it is soul not situation.

In Secret, my versions of Ritsos's short lyrics, was published in 2013. Since then, I have worked on some of the dramatic monologues, but had made sideways glances at 'Romiosini', aware of the fact that it's one thing to make versions from a language one doesn't speak (a method that might well provide the means to a poem in English that best represents the original) another to take on a poetic sequence whose purpose is not to speak of Greek identity, but Greek essence, a way of being Greek.

I read this poem at an event, held at the British Embassy in Athens, to mark the twentieth anniversary of Ritsos's death. My audience was made up almost entirely of Greeks: artists, composers, singers, musicians, writers. I read in the embassy reception hall where Thomas Phillips's portrait of Byron dressed in Albanian costume hung directly behind the podium that had been set for me. I opened by saying, 'Here I stand, a monolinguist reading my versions of Yannis Ritsos to a Greek audience, with Byron looking over my shoulder.' The reading went well. 'Romiosini Part Two' is under construction.

Romiosini Part One

Our trees look wrong in this shrunken sky
Our stones shift under these foreign feet
Our faces want only the heat of the sun
Our hearts want justice, justice, nothing more.

This reach of land's unyielding, hard as the silence.
It holds sun-broken rocks, it offers
abandoned olive trees and vines to the light,
to the light because there is only light, no water,
the road is lost in light, shadows are ironwork,
trees are stone, rivers are stone, our voices too are stone,
roots stumble on stone, stone-dust coats the leaves.

No water. Everyone thirsty. Everyone biting off
a mouthful of sky to choke down bitterness.
We are red-eyed from lack of sleep. Our faces
carry lines deep as the furrows cut in hillsides.
Our hands can't be prised from the gun, the gun
and the hand are the same thing, the gun and the hand
and the soul are the same thing. Hear our fury, see
the sorrow in our eyes: a star in a spillage of salt.

Our clenched fists summon the sun. Our smiles
are birds in flight. When we lie down to sleep
twelve stars drop from our pockets. When we die
the upward road is filled with flags and drums.

Year after year. No water. Everyone thirsty. Everyone
hungry. A bitter taste in the mouth. So many deaths.
Enemies coming by land, coming by sea.
Fields left bare to the sun, houses underwater,
doors broken down by the wind, a death-wind
blowing through the holes in our overcoats.

Dogs die wrapped in their shadows; the rain beats down on their bones.

We are stone men. We keep watch up here
on the heights. We smoke sheep-dung
mixed with the acrid leavings of the night. No bread,
no bullets. The gun and the heart are the same thing.
We keep watch as the sea builds waves that swamp the moon.

Year after year. Enemies coming by land, coming by sea.
Everyone thirsty, everyone hungry, so many deaths, yes,
but here we stand. Here is our flag of fire. And here
the flights of doves that leave our outstretched hands
at daybreak, bound for the skyline's open door.

JORGE EDUARDO EIELSON

Translated by Leonardo Boix

Jorge Eduardo Eielson (1924–2006) was not only a prolific poet, essayist, playwright and narrator, but also an accomplished visual artist, experimenting with sculpture, installation and photography. He is particularly known for his quipus, a reinterpretation of an ancient Andean device for recording information, consisting of brilliantly coloured threads knotted and tied in different ways. Eielson's quipus were exhibited in the 1964 Venice Biennale, and illustrated some of his most popular books, including his last poetry collection *Vivir es una obra maestra* (2003). He belongs to the *Generación del 50* of Peru, alongside Mario Vargas Llosa, Jorge Bacacorzo, and Julio Ramón Ribeyro, amongst others, and is widely considered one of the most influential Peruvian writers in the Latin American poetry of the second half of the twentieth century.

Although he was born in Lima and travelled widely in Peru, devoting himself to the study of pre-Columbian art, he moved to Italy in 1951, where he lived until his death in 2006. I came across Eielson's poems in 2014 while researching Latin American poets for my own first collection, and as there were hardly any available in English I embarked on translating some of his poems. That enriching process inspired me to respond to the translations, and I created my own variations of poems from *Vivir es una Obra Maestra* based on his wonderful imagery, sense of humour, plain, simple, everyday language and his masterful irony. These are presented here together with the Variations to the right of the translations. I understood his poems as literary quipus, knots of brilliant ideas and emotions. I never met Eielson, but through this complex and involved process of translation and interjection I felt I managed to converse with him. A humble homage to a poet barely known in the Anglo-speaking world, who I think deserves to be read more widely.

The Weight of the Planet: Variations on Eielson

Variations in Front of a Door

the door isn't closed
the door isn't closed or open
the door isn't open
the door is never closed
the door is never open or closed
the door is never open
the door has been closed for ever
the door is closed
the door has been open for ever
the door is open

The House of a Thousand Corridors

I closed the door,
touched the floor.
You said: 'I'm here'. We speak
to forget. The door is a door
of a house that we've been to.
It's now. And from there to the sea.
I said: 'Stay. I prepared maté'.
You open your eyes,
but we leave
anyway.

Dressed

Between a shoe and a glove
there are ties   jackets and
insolent trousers   there is a yellow gland
filling me with sweetness and wonder
There are tissues that smile
and tissues that die
There are smells   proteins and hats
a millions stars
in my temples
And dark cells
In my faeces
There are handkerchiefs too

The Green Socks

A painting by Magritte
at the Tate you once showed me.
We stood still, it was late.
I lied.
The room is a box without ears,
full of ties and neckties.
You are beside me, combing
    my hair
I go to sleep next to a pile:
my trousers, a pipe,
some socks,
silicon ear plugs

and hidden buttons
But above all there are ties
ties   there are ties

to stop the noise
filling the house.

Scales

It is just a ray
sourceless
Or perhaps a look
And I who live
With the light
Of a glass of water
In one hand
And all the weight
Of the planet
On another.

◆

The sky-blue glance
                    the pink skin
the whitest teeth

the black heart

◆

My heart has kept beating stupidly
since early on 13th April 1934.

All the Weight of the Planet

At 9 a.m. we went to the beach,
my clothes left behind,
you looked up at the sky,
I didn't notice
the icy sea
in my hands.

Just us
on the rocks,
bare feet.

◆

'Pray for me',
                    she said.
And then simply
                    died.

◆

My heart keeps beating stupidly.
I don't know when it started.

◆   ◆

Everybody asks me   Everybody asks me
how I can live a solitary life   how I can live a solitary life
on this sky-blue mountain   on this violet mountain

Nobody can see I am simply   Nobody can see I am simply
sitting on this chair   sitting on this chair
staring at an ordinary wall.   staring at an ordinary wall.

DIONISIO CAÑAS

Translated by Consuelo Arias

El gran criminal (The Outlaw) is a two-part poetic prose text narrated
in the voice of a marginalized subject, that of the urban Hispanic/
Latino writer. The poet's voice is that of a postmodern *flâneur*, a
descendant of Baudelaire's urban wanderer.

As well as Baudelaire, *El Gran criminal*'s literary forefathers
are the French 'Poètes Maudits', especially Rimbaud and Verlaine
whose oneiric verses and penchant for living on the edge have
influenced Cañas's poetry. Cañas's autobiographical voice is an
amalgam of marginal identities: the gay man, the outsider, the exile,
the Hispanic/Latino male inhabiting the nocturnal underworlds
populated by the various transgressive figures of New York – the
'city of night' par excellence – all moving to the rhythm of the *bolero*,
the sentimental song expressing the anguish of love and desire.

Dionisio Cañas is a border figure, residing between Latino New
York, Spain, and South America. Though born in Spain, he has lived
in New York City since the early seventies, deeply immersed in the
multi-Latino culture of the city. He is neither an Anglophone poet,
nor is he a Spanish poet, but rather, he is a Pan-Hispanic New York
poet. And it is precisely this that constitutes both his poetic voice (in
which he fuses the various modalities of the Spanish language) and
the space through which 'the outlaw' wanders.

The bilious hangover returns, as do the city's lights at dawn. The slow and spiralling passage of the hours, between ads for beer and cigarettes, whirls towards the eye of the storm; the hamburgers and the coffee whirl towards the eye; the smell of sweat and skin inflamed by lice whirls towards the eye; the hours, the hours, the hours happily whirl towards the eye.

Someone awaits you, someone awaits you, someone... Allow yourself the buzz of that first drink, allow life to pass you by, at once mundane and alien. Exile, what can you ask of time? You, the orphan of all orphans, you and the city, time spiralling, the night sky rising distant overhead as you wander through the avenues with circles under your eyes like birds lost in a labyrinth of temples, dives and bodegas. Only one image will save you: the glow of the streets at dawn, cleared of garbage from the night before.

◆

Thief, at night you prowl the city, you lie in wait for sunset so that these familiar streets might shroud you, a shadow among their shadows, a soul within their soul, the only pulse of your furtive love. Thief, you hunt in search of gleaming eyes, you catch the scent of fear rising in the throat, a bird of prey, you wander, you stalk in search of words, words that will bewitch, enthral, seduce, words that let you penetrate the Other with silken hand and steal the poem within and steal the words within his soul and make them yours. Thief, at night you prowl the city.

The vipers unleashed by drink and drugs are now asleep. Springtime. Morning in Manhattan. The breeze, an echo of the sea, sighs in his ear. The light rests on the treetops, while Ireland's flowers, silver sirens, blue, keep watch along the waterfront. Under the rain of images without a past forever lost the outlaw roams the streets. Writing his poem as he lives.

◆

Today I hate this city more than ever; tomorrow, as always, I'll love it once again. Its sounds, its sweat, its blood and semen find me. It invites us to share a table, though I know you are a story in a sea of stories. I've come to this bar where a perfume thief tells me of his shrewdness, but I prefer you, my waiter, you, disappearing into the Ninth Avenue night, withdrawing into the memories of your Island, your country, your weathered hut.

Mariano, metaphysician of Bronx bodegas, lover of salsa, rum and blow, charming sailor of the tango halls. You wield it like a pro, like a pecking beak, that credit card you use for making lines you snort through broken straws in sordid toilet stalls. You are a politico of the night who greets the dawn in lowlife bars, in those dives with sweet Latina barmaids. My good friend, my cruel reader, inhabitant of a city that festers light and slime, when will I see you again? So many times under the light we've seen a life wither neglected. Now, only the days and the hangovers remain, your mouth, your yellowed teeth, your nicotine scent and your white hair, your tongue, the language of your islands, your tattoo, all these things more enduring than desire... I love the fragility of stone, the moment when the impossible succumbs. That's why I wait. I press my lips to your ear to hear the murmur of your heart, the sounds of the city, the memory of your Island.

◆

When the shadows of the bar become familiar, and the scent of it, flesh of your flesh, when you hope the night will bring you only dreams, or a stampede of images you once loved or sweetly poisoned your days, when the rain falls on the streets like the hours on the heart, pointlessly and so dreadfully new, when your very name is blurred by drink... only then do you begin to understand your yearning for the simplicity of those days with him, as if they were the stars of a beautiful yet ordinary film. You leave the bar and its inhabitants; you don't look back in case a face, a word, brings back his name. You again recall that old love story you tell yourself when you're alone, when you become a shadow among shadows, searching for that breath with its scent of streets, searching for that vagabond body.

◆

NAKA TARŌ

Translated by Chikako Nihei and Andrew Houwen

Naka Tarō belonged to a Japanese generation that grew up during the Second World War and, as the conflict reached its dénouement, witnessed the widespread destruction of their cities. While 'Street Scene' and 'Trees' capture the sense of bitter endurance and privation of the early war years, 'Scene II' depicts what Naka saw when, at the age of twenty-four, his family home and his home city of Fukuoka were utterly devastated, though it also draws on the aftermath of the atomic bombs dropped on Hiroshima and Nagasaki.

Such experiences informed Naka's Buddhist-rooted understanding of life's impermanence. In 'Life', Naka first sought to come to terms with such impermanence. As the thirteenth-century Japanese essayist Yoshida Kenkō observed, it is because things are fleeting that they acquire their beauty. 'Life' both describes and itself enacts the consolation to be found in the beauty of impermanent things, as 'the dark sky that has lost everything | performs a requiem of dazzling tones'. It is through loss, Naka suggests, that we can discover the value of things.

Similarly, translation can seem at first to be a form of loss; and yet it is also in another sense a 'revival', as 'Life' has it, giving what Walter Benjamin calls a work's 'after-life'. In many ways the Buddhism that inspired Naka's poetry, with its understanding of the work of art's impermanence as it ceaselessly changes from one incarnation to the next, can provide fruitful ways of thinking about the process of translation itself.

Street Scene

in the hushed street
not even the sound of footsteps on the pavement
the shutters drawn down over all the windows

where has the murmuring leaves' gold dust gone?
where has the pale-faced woman consumed by illness
staring all day from a second-floor balcony vanished?

the reddish brown buildings   their doors nailed shut
now only the bones of branches piercing the chilly air

gods   now there is no one even to call your names

beyond the zinc roofs the endlessly open sea
on a tower an unseen flag flutters

Trees

dull   heavy
the earth under the undulating piles
of lead-coloured rubble
crushed   gasping
dark   dismal vacancy

ah   in this bitterly heavy scene
still persevering, the dusty trees!
already for so long
in the chinks of clouds, not a glimmer of light
in the air, not a breath of wind

emaciated naked trunks supporting
burnt-up brown diseased leaves
twisted branches bereft of birdsong

still enduring trees
existing, nothing more   on your own
how I choke when I look at you!

Scene II

summer 1945

the scabs of black memory tear off
the guillotine river cuts up
the city's torn skin

pushed along in the flow
countless burnt eyes
eyes
eyes

in the iridescent light
the guts of civilisation crumble like broken tiles
sticking out, a rib
a malleus
a thigh bone
nerve fibres tangled around them
like rusty phone wire

where are unravelled organs
sounding out again?

in the collapsed temple's hollowed eye-sockets
the illusion of poppies
burning silently

Life

time flows   in dreams   sunlight   appearances
in sight of the dying man the petals scatter   though there is no
wind
the sadly transparent cicada wings scatter

day by day what must be lost   sunlight   dreams
the delicate scent of the flowers   in a cry like remorse
the look in the loved woman's tearful eyes

nothing lasts a moment without breaking
waves of gold   spray of silver   in vain
the cruel roses scatter on the shore

the gathered red petals burn and pale
like a lost dream's reminiscence into the violet sea of illusion
a funeral wreath for the departed day

who can stop them   the colours of the disappearing clouds
ah   each day's endlessly repeated feast   who can say
fleeting yet therefore precious life   is empty

seek instead   for all fleeting phenomena
gathering day by day to dissolve deep into the spirit   into the heart
and revive in an irreplaceable song

as when   the dark sky that has lost everything
performs a requiem of dazzling tones

IVAN V. LALIĆ

Translated by Francis R. Jones

In late twentieth-century Yugoslavia, a 'great generation' of poets gained national and international acclaim. Their youth was marked by the harsh experience of the Second World War, and they were given full creative rein in the 1950s, when the Communist Party relinquished control over literature. Ivan V. Lalić (1931–1996) was one such poet.

The 1965 first issue of *Modern Poetry in Translation* featured two of his poems, translated from Serbian into English by Lalić himself. Several English-language collections have followed, some translated by Charles Simic and some by me. These trace his poetic development from his early blazing vividness of image to more measured and contemplative explorations, but with a sensuality throughout that is rooted in bodily experience – especially of the Mediterranean, which Lalić saw as his physical and cultural homeland. Key motifs in Lalić's poetry are the relationship between the seen, the felt, and the poet as seer, perceiver. Another theme is that of time, transience, and the fickle power of memory – including collective, cultural memory – to bridge them. Linking both is Lalić's meditative questioning of how far the word can both preserve and interpret the world.

Free verse dominates Lalić's 1960s–1980s work, which has been most translated. I'm now translating his 1992 collection *Pismo*, which I've called 'Letters'. Here, Lalić returns to traditional fixed forms. As this was an important poetic decision, I feel I need to respect it. That means transferring Lalić's forms into their best-fit English equivalents – rhymed hendecasyllables into rhymed iambic pentameters, say. However, Lalić is also a master of the straight-between-the-eyes poetic image, which it's crucial to respect too – such as, literally translated, 'the semantics of [rain]drops contains the shape of future gardens'. The conflict between these two pressures – form and meaning – can usually be resolved, though only after slow, painstaking work. Here, I eventually changed 'contains' to 'dream', a key word elsewhere in Lalić's poetry, so as to rhyme with 'scream' two lines later. What's important in such cases, I feel, is to stay faithful to Lalić's underlying poetic image, style and formal drive, even if the surface wording has to slide slightly at times.

Smile

I saw it glint like that gold death-
Mask from Mycenae, dust
Transformed: a smile of bated breath
Deep down in me had just

Condensed for a brief instant there,
Behind the mirror's glaze;
The future's pale unpupilled stare,
Impassive, held my gaze,

Like a house snake beneath the sill,
Mute, wise and unconcerned;
Though all is in its power, there's still
The pain of the return

To the dead centre, back to true,
The scales to zero, though
The years slant down and crumble to
An archipelago –

I've caught sight of my perfect twin,
Where this world's weight amasses,
And smile like Agamemnon in
The mirror's double glasses.

NOTE: 'House snake': in Serbian folk tradition, as in ancient Rome, a snake that came into a house would be fed bread and milk, and in return would act as the family's protector.

In Praise of Sleeplessness

Unsleeping eyes which do not only see
Wallpaper patterns and the morning's stain
Can read a future summer's history
Painstakingly hand-written by the rain –
For each leaf's destiny a single line
Attests to form: each drop's semantics dream
The future garden's shape, or the design
Of empty skies which sparkle, skies which scream.

The dreadful blessing of a waking night
Is felt when patience unbraids, from inside,
The eyes, then shifts the broadened roots of sight
To form new roads where new images ride –
A star is bursting into blooms of sea,
And in a glass of water, silence glitters,
Time after time your pasts keep breaking free,
No sea could taste as beautiful, as bitter.

Insomnia brings a fresh sleep into play:
Your waking self works on another plane –
Made in the old day's image, the new day
Has grown a shadow, so is not in vain;
You take your coat, your keyturn still ignites
The engine – acts exact but other-led –
Polysemy sings at the traffic lights,
Weaves a new fabric with three hues of thread...

All those who feel by night that time's unsure
Will give a different structure to their day,
From hour to hour; bound by its simple law,
They ask 'Is there a structure anyway?'
Insomnia spawns another sort of sleep:
The waking state which recreates you teems
With this new sleep, just as rainwaters seep
Through desert sands. And in it, freedom gleams –

For those who stay awake, nights are elsewhere,
A star is bursting into blooms of sea,
Primeval forests, choking, drink the air
And water of a summer still to be;
Last image: sleepless eyes, just like a rear-
View mirror filled with road as it's unrolled
To nothing, glimpse at Eden as they peer
Into the final sleeplessness, the fold.

Octaves on Summer

If a shadow hardens right at summer's start
And twines its way, like a vein in marble, through
This June, you know the summer will burst apart
Prematurely from inside, and split in two
Round Elijah's Day; twin powers with one heart
Still hold your once-taut threads; but they're releasing
Them now, emotionlessly, at increasing
Speed, while the fall's fatigue exacts its due.

Wind in the drained glass on the balcony slows
By early evening, settling to dregs of grit.
A butterfly in your heart. It seems you chose
To surrender your fall-back line, pawning it
For an absent mercy. On the road which flows
To the skyline, the gleam of distance is just
Starting to hem the dark, and the cloud of dust
Behind the rider who is bearing the writ.

Purple rags that flutter at dawn – all this
Is moving pictures, gardens tumbling downhill,
Towers plunging straight up into the abyss,
The upturned chalice overhead! It's a thrill
Which you've dressed up in words, like the imprecise
Future sensed by a prophet who doesn't know
How a slipshod imagination can grow,
Like contaminated wine, a haze of vice!

This will ripen into summer, perfecting
It when the Fates impassively ordain,
When future time and past, in their connecting
Vessels, both settle into a single plane.
Meanwhile the heart still keeps the herald in sight,
His winged heels, gauging their distance and speed –
And hears the wet cries of passing cranes recede
Into the fog and dark of their rain-soaked flight.

NOTE: The Orthodox feast-day of the Prophet Elijah falls
on the 2nd of August.

JOHN SMELCER

Translated by the author

The Ahtna Indians of Alaska live primarily along the Copper River.
The name of our culture and our language derives from the name of
the river, Atna' Tuu. As a member of the tribe and as one of the last
speakers of our severely endangered language (only about a dozen
elders still speak Ahtna; I am the only living member who can read
and write in Ahtna), I sometimes write or translate poems from
Ahtna into English. In the summer of 1982, during my summer break
from university, I got a job helping to map the Alaskan coastline
along the Arctic Ocean. It was quite an adventure. I was frequently
harassed by polar bears (the company issued me a rifle, which luckily
I never had to use). Flaxman Island is the northernmost island off
the coast of Alaska. One of my colleagues brought her portable kayak
to use during our downtime. It was during one of my kayaking
excursions that the events of this poem transpired. So far from home
for so many years and without another native speaker to talk to, I am
beginning to struggle to recall words. This may be the last poem I
ever translate from the Ahtna language. I hope I'm wrong.

The Polar Bear
Flaxman Island, Arctic Ocean, 1982

One time, when I was a young man
something remarkable happened to me.

I was paddling a kayak close to the seashore
when I saw a polar bear sitting on the ice looking

for something to eat. He was a big bear.
He jumped into the water and came after me.

Maybe he thought I was a giant seal.
He swam around my kayak three times.

I struck it with my paddle and shouted,
'Go away! Leave me alone!'

Finally, he swam back toward land.
I must have been blessed by Raven.

That is all there is to my story. Anyway,
I want to talk about something else now.

JOHANNES KÜHN

Translated by Simon Martin

I first came across Johannes Kühn's poems four or five years ago
when reading back through old editions of the *Jahrbuch der Lyrik*,
an anthology of contemporary poetry in German which appears every
two years (currently published by the Deutsche Verlags-Anstalt). I find
reading through anthologies can be an interesting way of comparing
and contrasting different tones and voices. In Johannes Kühn's case
I was struck by how his voice rang out, not through being strident,
but rather through its lucidity and musicality. To leap back across
the water, there is much that reminds me of Norman MacCaig's
later work – metrical freeness but an intense focus on cadence and
patterning so the lines feel right, flowing clausal sentences across line
ends, infrequent use of end rhyme, and a sense of place in the natural
world. And his handling of this subject is far from mawkish. He finds
joy and melancholy in the world around him, and views both with a
clear-eyed gaze which is not pulled or averted. There is a courage in
this which I find hopeful.

Turning Point

There's a thrum in the air,
soon the country will take flight
on blue wings.
Then,
a brown autumn toad,
the land will hiss
with its cold tongue.
But for now there is still
a loud violin song of bees,
September lanterns still shine as pears and apples
into the weakening light,
but for all that:
if only he would come, the angel, and take me captive,
take me away from all the ills which are to come.

Rainy Weather

Amused chuckles on the rooftops,
the rain lets the sound carry on across.
The spruces hiss
in green overcoats.
Their tips stab at drops
and shiver them, so that the water,
divided again and again, steams
as a wild summer current.

Fears that the drought will scorch
grass and corn to ash
flee from the heads
of all the farmers;
in doorways
they wave to each other.

Go, bring me my pipe,
I'll smoke for an hour
and be at ease
says an old man
to the grandchild
who has run into the yard
with an umbrella,
and is listening
to the drumming of its bright cloth.

The Weir

The jam of the drop walls, slap of the waters;
pulling firmly on the reins
quietness begins here
in waves like new blood;
and even the fish turn their bodies
more easily, celebrating
the flesh, laying down fat
beneath their smooth skins.

The needle pricks of dragonflies stitch
on a blue day a blue dress
for the water nymph
who comes at evening,
takes it away,
the same every summer's day.

A Shepherd

Right where he hangs his sleeping bag
on the branch of the apple tree
he stashes a well-wrapped package
of symphonies.
There, from amongst the branches
he takes them down
at a quarter to three
and plays some of them
on a tape recorder.

In the past on days like this
there was always an apple in the top of the tree
which he would knock down with his crook;
today he whisks himself off
to the concert halls of the world
and stands with his sheep
on the outskirts of the village,
hears the rain hissing
on his waterproof hat,
but the symphony
with its ringing instruments
wins out.

Overview

Stars
I have counted,
kicked up sand with my feet,
been involved in other nonsense.
I have sung of the fire of mullein flowers,
an oriole hitting its gong from the boughs.

At the time
friends reaped money, built houses,
brought home brides, and with their backs to me,
happy with their gardens,
happy with their children,
they now live.

Laughter from the village
floats over to me from its owners.

Yet I still have the velvet of the grass,
summer afternoon naps,
and I blow into my hands
out of pleasure.

But when winter turns my hair
the colour of snow
I am alone. Then –
crows, welcome
your deathly greeting,
dust, your blanket
soon over me,
end loneliness,
tower, toll soon
my way out of time.

BRONKA NOWICKA

Translated by Elżbieta Wójcik-Leese

Chestnut, sink, needle cushion, lump of clay and net curtain are five out of forty-four objects which lend their names and stories to forty-four prose poems or, as Bronka Nowicka prefers to call them, text modules collected in *To Feed the Stone* (2015). Only very few of these objects still exist (the needle cushion, made by Nowicka's grandmother, does) – most of them are remembered, with the help of the senses and language, 'to touch on what is human, not material'.

Nowicka is careful to clarify that her modules are not autobiographical. Their role is to document the images of objects we may hold in our memory, the images that may bring forth other images, for example, of the dead who may come to life thanks to the objects. The modules revolve around recollections, but these recollections have been modified too. 'I don't want dead objects to be alive; I want alive people to be less dead.'

The most important object is the stone found by the girl, the child protagonist whose perspective organizes Nowicka's book. 'The child believes that she can feed the stone with her senses ... She shows it the world,' explains Nowicka. 'The tragic – because impossible – relationship between the child and the stone is pivotal to the book, which also deals with complicated family life, emotional and physical violence, ageing, death, illness, madness, sadness. It's a heavy book. But it also has a bright side: the child's belief in the possibility of feeding the stone.'

For Nowicka as an interdisciplinary artist, language – 'kinetic, synesthetic, sensual' – is the best narrative tool, the medium which can adhere to our thinking without any intermediary. She realizes the impossibility of coming to know and expressing the whole world, yet she chooses to adopt Henri Michaux's approach: 'I have seven or eight senses. One of them: an absence.' For her, writing is feeding her own and other people's absences.

Teaspoon

The dead take sugar only when we push teaspoons into their hands and we ourselves make circles in the bottom of their cups. Then the sugar crystals pretend to be tornadoes. These whirlwinds put the tea leaves on merry-go-rounds, whirling, though the teaspoons, propped against the saucers, have already cooled down. Let there be movement. Let an ant escape across the tablecloth, lugging a crumb of cake. We need a wasp over the table. Let something buzz. It will disarm the silence of this scene, before the dead speak the language glued for them from thin paper strips of saved-up words. Before we hide behind their backs and start speaking for them, imagining they move their lips. Later we'll guide their fingers over the plates, with their help we'll crumble biscuits, collect the crumbs on their fingertips, which we ourselves will lick. In the end, tired with the weight of these puppets, we'll put their hands on their knees, signalling the end of both afternoon tea and a memory.

The dead do not get dressed by themselves. We do it for them. Combing hair, shaving, sliding a pin into the hair and a link into the cuff. Putting wood into the stove, taking off the kettle when it whistles.

We need to clean their shoes. Lick stamps and send letters, which do not reach us. They won't think what we haven't thought for them, so they think of us with our own thoughts.

They happen to sit in the heat with gloves and woollen hats on. Or in hats made of snow – over a frozen river where we forgot them last spring.

The child leaves her grandfather over a cup of tea. Tomorrow she'll come to sweeten it again. And again, until the sugar of the whole world runs out.

Chestnut

The child dreams about a landscape that tells lies. She looks at the leaves: they're sewn to the trees. Dogs stand next to their kennels, since their paws are dug into the ground. Who saw such flocks of sparrows sitting on the ground? Throw something and they won't fly away. Run into them – they won't take wing, you can nail their heads with your feet.

The child walks down to the river of things, which accepts everything and returns nothing. Objects float. Photographs: face up, like dead fish, belly up. The people in these portraits took water into their mouths, learnt how to breathe with gills that had grown at the back of their heads, on the brims of their hats, on the plaits brushed to their backs.

Needles. Shoals of rusty needles. Spools of thread. A thimble. Tables pull along Sunday tablecloths, the river sucks starch out of them, dilutes vodka, steals bread. Dolls: whole, headless, dressed or naked.

The darned pocket of the jumper tosses out a chestnut – it pulls towards the sleeve as if expecting a hand to stop it. The chestnut resembles a stone.

Each object in this river searches for its hand, each person on the bank searches for their thing. You can't walk into the water, you can only look. The child will wait here until she wakes. Maybe she'll see what once she knew only by touch, and now only by name.

Sink

Our father is growing up. Not because mother has started to shave him and she's buying him bigger shoes, but because he wants to go out into the world. Except he doesn't know how to. He puts away thinking about it, though he's already trying on a body suitable for the occasion.

He stands in front of the mirror and wears down his comb too fast. He may think the direction of his combing will also set the course for other things. He makes a parting as if he created a planet. Destroys it and a new planet is born. More to the left.

After building numerous inferior worlds, father succeeds on the head of the proper one, puts the comb down and rests. Then he proceeds to smooth out his belly, but his hands are too small to iron so much skin. They look like doll hands attached with rubber bands to the buttons of shirt sleeves.

Sensing that he can't do more than what has been done, father rises on his tiptoes and walks to the door. It doesn't want to open, though his elbow pushes the door handle down with all its might.

Mother is washing a pot, and father is watching the stream being sucked into the vortex at the bottom of the sink. He envies it: it can run away from home. He, too, would love to vanish down the drain, clutching to something so small that together they would squeeze through the metal eyelet. He sees himself floating in a warm shell of the drained pasta, clinging on to an apple stalk by his fingernails. But in the greasy sink there's nothing except water. And water cannot be caught.

Needle Cushion

The child is sad because she cannot feed the stone. Not because she can't find its mouth. She knows it's all mouth. She doesn't know what to put the stone next to so the stone wants to eat it.

She goes into the kitchen to ask for the chipped saucer used by the cat. She pulls at her mother's apron, once, twice. This is how she knocks on the door of her mother's attention. It opens, for a moment cut out of the chopped meat. The child is pointing at the saucer, all request.

'Take it.'

Mother is back to beating the board with the knife. She beats in double time.

'Don't hurt yourself.'

She does it even before she steps over the threshold. She has pressed her thumb too hard against the glass chip. She's collected some blood into the cat's saucer.

Now she is carrying the stone. With the same caution she carried only the fledgling. She kneels down and puts the stone on the saucer's rim. She prods it gently, like a blind animal, so that it moves over to where the blood lies. It rolls and clots. Wouldn't budge.

The child asks for a cushion. The cushion that belonged to the needles, and now belongs to no one, aged and pricked. At night, when there's darkness, she puts the stone on the cushion. She offers the stone bread skin. Lies down beside it. Waits.

The white next to the skin – the flesh of bread – is the only thing that shines. The child knows, somehow, that night is heavy, it weighs heavily on every object: coal in the bucket, button, thread, eyelid. Night holds scales weights. The bread skin keeps on shining, untouched.

The child cannot sleep. Scared that she won't notice when the stone dies. That she will carry in her hand the dead, speak to the dead, lie in bed with the dead. She's afraid it will die because it doesn't eat.

'Mum.'

She mustn't wake her mother, on whom night has put its weight.

Lump of Clay

The child put the stone next to many things, but none became smaller. Because they kept exactly the same amount of themselves, it meant they were inedible.

Then the child found the hollow under her tongue and placed the stone inside. She herself didn't grow heavier. She felt that she was less. Not the kind of less when you become less, because you live and use up life. The kind of less when you give something of yourself.

The child strolled across the garden and looked at what it was. The stone was eating this view together with the child, who'd already realized: she could feed the stone with whatever came through her senses. Even with a lump of clay, if she looked at it, or plain grass, if she touched it. Maybe even with the very thought of grass.

Net Curtain

Sunday is a quiet retarded girl in white knee-high socks. With a chiffon bow at the end of her mousey plait. They pin a cherry brooch to her hat, don't stint on ice creams, she needs some target for her overgrown tongue. They push a twig with catkins into her hand. Let her wave it round as she's singing: ho-ho. And a hankie folded in three. Handy in the church, when she kneels, not to stain her knees.

And all Sunday wants to do is to stare at funerals. She conducts them with her twig – they need to know how to proceed. They multiply, as if mourning were a plague.

The smallest funeral procession consists of the hearse and the lamenting man: the old mare is pulling a cart with the child, the father walks behind. Thinks that he's buried dreams so young. The sun is shining. Funeral processions pass one another. Hats are tipped. Mourners watch to compare whose horse is the healthiest. Horses glance from behind their blinkers to compare whose coffin is the prettiest, in which life looks alive. Some hurry to get to the wake.

At the wake chicken soup and polished spoons. The world mirrored in them so nicely, though upside down. Dill sprinkled on potatoes like green snow. Radio buzzes like a bee. Wind puffs up the starched net curtain.

'Ho-ho,' says Sunday, 'ho-ho.'

BERTOLT BRECHT

Translated by Tom Kuhn

It is not very often that a new poem by Brecht turns up. This early piece arrived in the Berlin Brecht Archive in 2016, nearly a century after it was written, by way of childhood friends and middle-men. It is a draft, written in pencil with several corrections, on a single folded sheet.

Brecht was often inclined to speak of himself in the first person, and not only as a young man. We have only to think of the testaments and conclusions to his two greatest collections: 'Of poor B.B.', which ends *The Domestic Breviary*, and 'To those born after', the final poem of *Svendborg Poems*. So we can think of this piece as a first foray in this direction, an essay in self-revelation and concealment, a first act to this play of selves. We have no reason to doubt the first line, in which case the verses date from the early months of 1918. He had already begun to call himself 'Bertolt', but here, on the cusp, he still uses the spelling handed down by the family. This was also when Brecht discovered Villon, and here he models himself on an image of the fifteenth-century bandit and ballad-singer in a kind of idealised autobiography: he has not, admittedly, suffered like his hero (who features in the third stanza), but he still asserts his right, like Villon in his 'Testament', to protest.

The poem ends with a colon. Was it perhaps meant to continue? Or was this not rather by way of acknowledgement that these stanzas were just a prologue? We have an announcement: the arrival of a new kid and of a new edgy, angry, truculent voice. He doesn't perhaps know yet what he wants to say, but by God he knows he wants to say it! And so the tone and *Gestus* of much of the young Brecht is anticipated here. We see germs of some of *The Domestic Breviary* (1927) and maybe even of *The Threepenny Opera* (1928). Quite a find then, and well worth having an English version.

I, Berthold Brecht . . .

1

I, Berthold Brecht, just turned twenty
Brown of hair and weak of eye
Born in Augsburg on the river
Not so much cheeky, rather shy,
I, who've never had to beg
Of life who've felt but little pain
Been coddled like a new-laid egg
Notwithstanding, I complain.

2

There's no point getting cross about it:
Sometimes a man must have relief.
Just sign your names and while you're at it
Give me benediction, not grief.
And as there isn't – more's the pity –
I'll start by getting this off my chest:
That there's no qualified authority
To whom one properly should protest.

3

As long ago a poor stray sinner
Born in Paris of parents crust-less
Wrote in the unfeeling winds
His bitter song of life's injustice
– The man himself was dead soon after
Five centuries since have been and went
Yet no one ever did discover
If anything came of his lament!

4

So I, before old age takes hold
Dims my sight and stops my mirth
Teaches me humility and, when I'm cold
Gently pushes me under the earth,
With no particular addressee
I'll hurl into the winds once more
Not meekly, nor on bended knee
The following refusal to concur:

© Stiftung Akademie der Künste, Berlin

ARIANE DREYFUS

Translated by Olivia McCannon and Susan Wicks

SUSAN WICKS: These poems are all taken from Ariane Dreyfus'
most recent collection (2013), *Le dernier livre des enfants (The Children's
Last Book)*. The centre-justified poems are part of a series placed at
intervals and based on Richard Hughes' 1929 novel, *A High Wind in
Jamaica*, and its 1965 film adaptation by Alexander Mackendrick.

The critic Matthieu Gosztola has likened Ariane Dreyfus' poetry
to a language of 'nakedness, a nakedness confided to us in whispers,
crystallised into poems'. For me, the biggest challenge of translating
this apparently simple, transparent language was to resist the
temptation of over-interpreting, to respect the originals' moments of
ambiguity, their mystery and restraint. Dreyfus' 'simplicity' can leave
much unsaid. The poems in *Le dernier livre des enfants* are rich with
meanings. Her own blurb for the book ends with this: 'It was time for
me to risk myself nearer the edge. Not a bird, no. But as I was and as
we still are, astonished at having hardly moved at a time when we can
already see death.'

OLIVIA MCCANNON: In her essay, *La poésie quand nous la faisons* (2012),
Dreyfus tells us: '...I often come back to childhood, as you might dip
your paintbrush into water to keep on painting...' That confluence
of water and childhood runs, ever further and deeper, through the
Le dernier livre des enfants. Dreyfus plunges in, curious, attentive, to its
wonders and terrors, and comes out more alive.

Her line, irreducible, counters all kinds of solitude with its hope,
and human presence. Here is a writer who writes to be *with*, for whom
poetry is 'surely a sister to friendship, the only human bond of any
importance'. Her generosity breathes warmth wherever it turns to
look: at death, neglect, abuse.

In the same essay, Dreyfus writes: 'I watch the sky less than the big screen.' The cinema is a place to look at the faces of women – actors, existing, making other stories possible, 'as if I'm before a magic mirror that ultimately gives back something of my own face, that I'll never see.' I felt something equally heartening as I translated these poems of hers.

Inside

Because it goes everywhere pain is like water

In the kitchen she comes into
The little boy has set his cup down on the floor
By the dog, stays to stroke him

Both without a word

One asleep on his side the other nestling in
Leaning his head

'Are you tired my sweet?'

The dog lifts up, wagging its tail, then puts its head back down on
    crossed paws. The tail keeps thudding the ground, eager to please.
The sound makes the child she'd thought asleep burst out laughing.
    From below,
His little fingers find a way to link into hers.

She looks around her, everything reappears

The faded flowers
Of the waxed cloth, so often wiped
The red and green check
Of the apron thrown over the chair
Pot open the jam shines

When she looks down the dog
Is licking the boy's temple, feelingly

Why did she believe in a stop to their days?

OM

The Happiness We Can

Open sea

I plunge my head forwards
Interested in the first fish
Whose eye will meet mine

Swimming

On my belly
As it does
Arriving as several

We whirl we whirl
Who is whose sibling?

Seven fish opening mouths
Crossing the water swallowing
Infinitesimal food
Whatever's shredded

If I meet one on its own
Remembering a fear of straying
I stick close to one of my kind
Who like another
Dives down to the sand-blurred light

Belly throbbing I sought
Less pain by moving
Diving back in

Of these traces that were me
Not one is left in the water
Swimming where they go, I play
At living
In the sea as several

Escaping from my shadow
Faster still

If my arm is reaching out

OM

The Dolls are All Here...

The dolls are all here
Wood, metal
Rags, she gathers them up

Rachel little sister
All that is carried, falls
A rope-end
Greasy she picks it up
Hugs it tightly to her
Everything is so important
The marlin spike sharp enough to split
A skull if it fell
Slips a little in her arms
She's holding the mast you see
Showing the world
To her youngest son
Then brings him down sharpish
He's so sleepy
Tucks him in he's so cold
And suddenly touches with her hand
A miserable rag
Another poor baby
We must find her a roof
Or a deep crack
Or walls, at the very least a parasol
She stops to think for a moment
Would she rather go in
This is where the door would be
Would she rather go out

If she's called
Little open jar
Yes she can see him wailing
She's looking right at him
Rachel loves to walk
In the right direction
So much to do
So many families
On this ship
All over the place she's stowed them
If you want a cup of tea
Don't forget your children
You have to sing them little songs you know

Or they'll all start crying

OM

The Alzette

Have the steps sunk?
That final tread
Touching the water, goes out alone
Even by day the river is so dark

The water no longer flows

Where the step leans out I believe it alive
I've come back to see it

So smooth in its stone become eyes with their lids drawn down

Laid in its place in the world

It goes out alone, save a slight, frail branch of pink lilac
Settling under the rain
My palm cups the blossom
Holding still, then heavy
When the cluster yields the smell alone is overpowering

I would have liked to sit down
Folded in like childhood
But not just that
The step already in the water
Would teach me to descend

So far, only the lilac has wet my hand

We don't enter we disappear into death

Far more transparent
Than the water

That innocently slides into the prettiest of names

OM

NOTE: The Alzette river flows through the city of Luxembourg
and between deep winding gorges.

One of Them

Tickled by the string behind his neck, he feels his head
    to check his Indian feathers
Then rests his hand on the chair-back to reflect

In the tepee, standing there to wonder
If the others are all dead
Should he think of them their names,
Should he dream up a survivor's song?

He moves towards the curtain, nothing else to fill the afternoon
The wounded chief is lying in the white men's prison
The chief's son has set his foot at the river's edge, the horse
Is taking a long drink
And he's the one who also saved their young girl's life

Her dress is moving
He watches her crying, can't make up his mind

The curtain partly open so you can look out
On the poplar trees, the ring-road traffic doesn't
Shake a single one

The wrist he's leaning on, not moving, starts to hurt
He won't call anyone
He can make his own pain move from place to place
With his eyes shut trace it like a trail

And I, in writing, I'm not leaving anyone
The way I pass

SW

On The Road

Slowly downwards from his shoulder the snail

The little boy says nothing, arm laid squarely on his thigh, as he protects
    the creature's progress with a finger

The child curls his body round to open his other hand
If the snail were to fall, he'd pick it up
And yet
It isn't power, it's grief

That swells inside him, touches his belly's edges

It's too much, this being carried off, not choosing
In a car it's worse, he doesn't even know why foot by foot he's being
   torn away

When he picks up the snail to lift it closer to his face its graceful horns
   go frantic
And instead of touching him the way he wanted disappear
Inside the stationary shell

He could throw it, a long way, out of the car window
Miles from here, a gesture, show that he is free

Except the shell's not empty – light, but empty, no

This tiny weight in the palm of his hand is nothing less than life
The only thing that's capable of saying close-up in his ear:
Hello, you

SW

Emily Searches with Her Eyes...

Emily searches with her eyes
For the eyes of the little monkey
He'll jump up again, stone dead

Old captain, but she's old
As well, she's ten years old
Runs on the sliding boat
Her dress no longer looks like anything
She's got her skin to live in
Once her strap slipped down
He started back
But the picture moves
In several lights
If it's at night
He's pulling up on her
The blanket that's slipped off
Soaked through with fever
Sometimes opening her eyes
To watch the porthole
On the plate the knife
Moves too it hurts
Her leg hurts it won't let her eat
He gives her pictures
Sea-tossed pirates
Only they're the truth
And he's the captain
In the cabin where she moans
She's breathing in advance
The memory of her whole life

Wherever she could go
She's been to see and look
The sky the wind old face
In front of her young face
You don't say love
Because the space of time's too big
And sudden cowardice
Will speed up death
The boat would cradle her
When she used to sleep up there
Against the mast squeezed tight
Between her legs
And in her arms
That's all

The small black pig says nothing
All too well
Snout buried in an armpit

Too worn out even to stretch
Because of the sun that's beating on her head
And everyone's
Even the bubbling pitch between the joints
Emily does as he does
Sighs and says nothing
The little pig can go on making
Her his living bed
It's all he lives for in his innocence
On the deck where the children
Try sleeping anywhere they can
If she goes farther to the edge of shade

Because today the sun is crazy
When she moves the faint cries go with her
In a little feverish pile
Of meat that's waiting to be eaten
She scratches her cheek
For feeling touched has made her itch
There's only this young pig
Between death, in any case, and her
Half-open eye
The pirates are all there
Sitting cross-legged to repair the sails
Sliding across the deck as they are done
All crushed on top of one another, and a crab
Escaping and then lost but not for long, recaught
The men are laughing, they are lying on the ground
Rolling about laughing
Emily likes them
But it's starting to be a long time now
Inside her mouth
She casually flips her tongue
To give the walled-up prisoner a time to play
And go tock tock or could it be the swell
That's crushing her ribs a bit
The little piglet shudders in his dream
Like an offer of escape that comes to nothing

Even if the ocean doesn't swallow us we'll still be swallowed up

SW

FRIEDRICH HÖLDERLIN

Translated by David Constantine

In the two poems published here, both rewritten and expanded in the summer of 1800 from earlier versions, the beloved woman is Susette Gontard, wife of a Frankfurt banker whose personal motto was 'Les affaires avant tout' (business first). Hölderlin's poetic name for Susette was Diotima, the woman in Plato's *Symposium* who taught Socrates the philosophy of love when he was young.

Home

> The boatman comes home glad to the still river
> From distant islands when he has harvested;
> So I should come home too had I as
> Much good harvested as I have sorrow.
>
> Dear riverbanks, once my fosterers, can you
> Still the sorrows of love, can you promise me,
> Woodlands that I was young in, when I
> Come back to you my peace of mind again?
>
> The cool beck where I watched the ripples playing,
> River where I watched the ships gliding away
> There I'll soon be, the familiar hills
> Who were my guardians once, the homeland's

Revered and safe frontiers, my mother's house,
   Sister and brother, their loving embraces,
      I will enjoy and they'll enfold me
         And swaddle my heart in healing bands for

They have kept faith with me. But I know, I know
   The sorrow of love will not be healed so soon,
      No lullaby that a consoling
         Human sings will sing it away from me.

For those who lend us heaven's fire, the gods,
   They give us the gift of holy sorrrow too.
      So be it. I'm a son of the earth
         Made, as it seems, to love and to suffer.

Parting

So intending to part, thinking it good and wise
  Why did the doing it shock us like murder then?
    How little we know ourselves!
      Working in us there's a god

Whom to betray, creator for us at the start
  Of sense and life, inspiriter and guardian
    Angel of our love, only
      That I don't have the strength to do.

Worldly sense however has other rules of wrong
  Practises other strict service, another code
    And day by day convention
      Filches the living soul from us.

Oh I knew this already! Since between the gods
  And humans, fear, that deformity, rooted
    Lovers must die and blood must
      Flow from their hearts in atonement.

Let me be silent, let me never again view
  This killing thing but in peace may I go away
    From here into loneliness
      So the parting still be ours.

Hand me the cup yourself so that of the saving
    Sacred poison, the Lethe drink, I drink enough
        With you and love and hatred
            Will all of it be forgotten.

I shall leave. Perhaps a long while hence I'll see you
    Diotima here. But desire by then will be
        Bled white and peacefully like
            The blessed as strangers we shall walk

Conversation leading us, pensive, hesitant
    To and fro until here the place of the parting
        Alerts our forgotten selves
            Warmth comes into our hearts again

I look at you amazed, I hear voices, sweet songs
    As from a former age, the playing of a lute
        And the lily lifts, fragrant
            Golden, over the stream to us.

WAR OF THE BEASTS AND THE ANIMALS

Focus on Russian and Ukranian Poetry

ILYA KAMINSKY

From 'Barometers'

1.

My family huddled by the doorframe at 4 a.m., debating whether or not to open the door to the stranger wearing only his pyjama bottoms, who'd been pounding on the door for at least five minutes, waking the whole apartment complex. Seeing the light come on, he began shouting through the door.

'Remember me? I helped you haul your refrigerator from Pridnestrovie. Remember? We talked about Pasternak on the drive. Two hours! Tonight they bombed the hospital. My sister is a nurse there. I stole someone's truck and drove across the border. I don't know anyone else. Can I make a phone call?'

So the war stepped its shoeless foot into my childhood two decades ago, under the guise of a half-naked man gulping on the phone, victim of an early post-Soviet 'humanitarian aid' campaign.

2.

During a recent visit to Ukraine, my friend the poet Boris Khersonsky, and I agreed to meet at a neighbourhood café in the morning to talk about Pasternak (as if he is all anyone talks about in our part of the world). But when I walked up the sidewalk at 9 a.m., the sidewalk tables were overturned and rubble was strewn into the street from where the building had been bombed.

A crowd, including local media, was gathered around Boris as he spoke out against the bombings, against yet another fake humanitarian aid campaign of Putin's. Some clapped; others shook their heads in disapproval. A few months later, the doors, floors, and windows of Boris's apartment were blown up.

There are many stories like this. They're often shared in short, hurried sentences, and then the subject is changed abruptly.

How can one speak about, write about, war? 'Truthful war books', Orwell wrote, 'are never acceptable to non-combatants.'

[...]

3.

Over the last twenty years, Ukraine has been governed by both the Russian-speaking East and the Ukrainian-speaking West, united in just one thing: corruption. The government periodically uses 'the language issue' to incite conflict and violence, an effective distraction from the real problems at hand. The most recent conflict arose in response to the inadequate policies of President Yanukovych, who has since escaped to Russia. Yanukovych was universally acknowledged as the most corrupt president the country has ever known (he'd been charged with rape and assault, among other things, all the way back to Soviet times). However, these days, Ukraine's new oligarchical government is composed of politicians whose CVs might remind one of Bernie Madoff's.

When the standoff between the Yanukovych government and crowds of protesters first began in 2013, and the embattled President left the country shortly thereafter, Putin sent his troops into Crimea, a Ukrainian territory, under the pretext of passionately protecting the Russian-speaking population. Soon, the territory was annexed. In a few months, under the pretext of humanitarian aid, more Russian military forces were sent into another Ukrainian territory, Donbas, where a proxy war has begun.

All along the protection of Russian language was continually cited as the sole reason for the annexation and hostilities.

Does the Russian language in Ukraine need this protection? In response to Putin's occupation, many Russian-speaking Ukrainians chose to stand with their Ukrainian-speaking neighbours, rather than against them. When the conflict began to ramp up, I received this e-mail:

I, Boris Khersonsky, work at Odessa National University where I have directed the department of clinical psychology since 1996. All that time I have been teaching in Russian, and no one has ever reprimanded me for 'ignoring' the official Ukrainian language of the state. I am more or less proficient in the Ukrainian language, but most of my students prefer lectures in Russian, and so I lecture in that language.

    I am a Russian language poet; my books have been published mostly in Moscow and St. Petersburg. My scholarly work has been published there as well. Never (do you hear me – NEVER!) did anyone go after me for being a Russian poet and for teaching in Russian language in Ukraine. Everywhere I read my poems in RUSSIAN and never did I encounter any complications. However, tomorrow I will read my lectures in the state language – Ukrainian. This won't be merely a lecture – it will be a protest action in solidarity with the Ukrainian state. I call for my colleagues to join me in this action.

[...]

4.

Every poet refuses the onslaught of language. This refusal manifests itself in silence illuminated by the meanings of poetic lexis – the meanings not of what the word says, but of what it withholds. As Maurice Blanchot wrote, 'To write is to be absolutely distrustful of writing, while entrusting oneself to it entirely.'

    Ukraine today is a place where statements like this one are put to the test. Another writer, John Berger, says this about the relationship of a person to one's language: 'One can say of language that it is potentially the only human home.' He insisted that it was 'the only dwelling place that cannot be hostile to man . . . One can say anything to language. This is why it is a listener, closer to us than any silence or any god.' But what happens when a poet refuses his language as a form of protest?

[...]

5.

On another visit to Ukraine, I saw a former neighbour of mine, now a war-cripple, holding his hand out on the street. He wasn't wearing any shoes. As I hurried by, hoping he wouldn't recognize me, I was suddenly brought up short by his empty hand. As if he were handing me his war.

As I walked away from him, I had an eerie feeling of recognition. How similar his voice, the voices of the Ukrainian poets I've been speaking with, to the voices of people in Afghanistan and Iraq, whose houses my own tax money has destroyed via USA's own 'humanitarian aid' excursions.

7.

What exactly is the poetry's witness? The language of poetry may or may not change us, but it shows the changes within us. Like a seismograph, it registers the violating occurrences. Miłosz titled his seminal text *The Witness of Poetry* 'not because we witness it, but because it witnesses us'. Living on the other side of the Iron Curtain, Zbigniew Herbert told us something similar: a poet is like a barometer for the psyche of a nation. It cannot change the weather. But it shows us what the weather is like.

8.

Can examining the case of a lyric poet really *show* us something that is shared by many – the psyche of a nation? The music of a time?

How is it that a lyric poet's spine trembles like a barometer's needle? Perhaps this is because a lyric poet is a very private person: in her or his privacy this individual creates a language – evocative enough, strange enough – that enables her or him to speak, privately, to many people at the same time.

9.

Living many hundreds of miles from Ukraine, away from this war, in my comfortable American backyard, what right do I have to write about this war? And yet I cannot stop writing about it: cannot stop mulling over the words by poets of my country in English, this language they do not speak. Why this obsession? Between sentences is the silence I do not control. Even though it is a different language, the silence between sentences is still the same: it is the space in which I see a family still huddled by the doorframe at 4 a.m., debating whether or not to open the door to the stranger, wearing only his pyjama bottoms, who is shouting through the doorframe.

This is an excerpt from Ilya Kaminsky's essay which is published fully in *Words for War: New Poems from Ukraine* (forthcoming from Academic Studies Press, Boston http://www.academicstudiespress.com/forthcoming/wordsforwar Readers of *MPT* will receive a $5 discount on this book by entering the code MPT-WORDS at checkout.

KATERYNA KALYTKO

Translated by Olena Jennings and Oksana Lutsyshyna

In Kateryna Kalytko's poetry beautiful images come together like pieces of a puzzle to create violent and shocking images of war and an atmosphere depicting the sense of loss and pain that is experienced during a search for safety and identity in violent times.

The challenge was to render the emotional temperature of Kateryna Kalytko's poetry. She is – for the English-speaking world – very, very emotional. In Ukrainian, Kalytko uses a lot of approximate rhymes (Ukrainian, unlike English, is rich that way – with plenty of precise rhymes available, since it is a highly inflected language). But Kateryna chooses (and acts as a bit of a trend-setter in this regard) approximate rhymes, as if to show that nothing we know we really know, nothing is precise, and we approach life only by approximation. Her approximate rhymes, to us, are a sign of humility and deep understanding of the connectedness of things.

Another challenge was in the rhyme itself. Rhyme is not so common for poetry in English, especially poems on serious, difficult topics, such as war, violence and grief. And yet, to strip Kateryna Kalytko's poems of rhymes completely also seemed wrong. We agreed that it would be best to preserve a small number of rhymes, and to compensate for the losses inevitable in poetry translation by formal means: by sometimes breaking the stanzas into smaller ones, or changing the length of a line. This way, the rhymes, by suddenly appearing, punctuate the text, arrest the readers' attention, and emphasize the tragic nature of the events and feelings of the poem. The contrast of beautiful and violent images creates dense, emotional poetry in which the writer becomes a refugee in search of shelter and identity at the time of war.

They Won't Compose Any Songs...

They won't compose any songs, because the children of their children,
hearing about this initiation, will jump out of their beds at 4 a.m.,
    frightened
by the echo in their spinal cords. Separate parts of death
cannot form a whole: a quarter of fate or of body is always missing.
The map is worn at the folds.

The doors of the house rust hopelessly, you are on night watch.
At dawn saliva becomes poison in every mouth.
All these piles of ashes still have names
and they keep repeating their persistent calls
sharp like panicked bird shrieks, too extreme for a song
about a field torn apart by a hail of bullets,
about the *chornozem* that God will rub off in his hand afterwards.

This Loneliness Could Have a Name...

This loneliness could have a name, an Esther or a Miriam.
Regiments fall to the ground with an infant's cry.
Words hardly fit between water and salt.
Under the flag at half-mast, hundreds of hoarse voices

laugh, pricked by the splinters of language.
This loneliness is vast, bottomless, and so chilling
that even a stranger turns away. Restless children wander
out of the school, stand by the sea, as if in front of a tribunal.

Dried tree branches crackle in the air like transmitters.
Somebody keeps calling out the name of the city turned into ashes.
This loneliness could be named Sevgil or Selima.
The names of the abandoned are salty and deep.

She comes out, fumbles with the knot
of her black headscarf; her lips are pale.
Who is there, she says, do you read me? Does anyone hear us?
Just a moment ago somebody called out our names.

Do you read me, son, try and listen to me, to me –
they have all left the shore, look for them in the sea.

Home Is Still Possible There...

Home is still possible there, where they hang laundry out to dry,
and the bed sheets smell of wind and plum blossoms.
It is the season of the first intimacy
to be consummated, never to be repeated.
Every leaf emerges as a green blade
and the cries of life take over the night and find a rhythm.

Fragile tinfoil of the season when apricots first form
along with wars and infants, in the same spoonful of air,
in the stifling bedrooms or in the cold, from which the wandering
beg to enter, like a bloom of jellyfish, or migratory blossoms.
The April frost hunts white-eyed, sharp-clawed,
but the babies have the same fuzzy skin for protection.

What makes them different is how they break
when the time comes for them to fall, or if they get totally crushed.
Behind the wall a drunken one-armed neighbour stumbles around
    his house,
confusing all the epochs, his shoulder
bumps into metal crutches from WWI, a Soviet helmet made of
    cardboard,
and the portrait of a man with a glance like a machine gun firing
and hangers for shirts, all of them with a single sleeve.

So they will fall and break into pieces and fates
branches parted, fruit exposed to the winds.
The neck feels squeezed, in the narrow isthmus of the throat
time just stands still and mustard gas creeps through the ditches.

All of this is but a forgotten game we play in the family backyard,
hiding amongst the laundry that hangs outside
the world becomes more fragile at each moment, and when you
    suddenly embrace
through the cloth – you don't know who it is, and whether you've lost
    or found.

And the swelling parted body of war intrudes into a blossoming heart
because we didn't let it enter our home on a cold night to warm itself.

These poems by Kateryna Kalytko are taken from *Words for War:
New Poems from Ukraine* (forthcoming from Academic Studies
Press, Boston
http://www.academicstudiespress.com/forthcoming/wordsforwar
Readers of MPT will receive a $5 discount on this book by entering
the code MPT-WORDS at checkout.

BORIS KHERSONSKY

Translated by Ostap Kin, Polina Barskova, Olga Livshin and
Andrew Janco

To readers interested in understanding the psychology of a certain kind of
post-Soviet Russian thinking that contributes to the war in Ukraine, Boris
Khersonsky's work is indispensable. It frames the war within the larger
context of millennia-old imperial ambition and the myopic patriotism of
empire's citizens, and it treats these destructive phenomena with urgency.

To accomplish this, Khersonsky borrows certain elements from
Joseph Brodsky's seminal work. Like Brodsky, he avoids open emotional
expression; both poets place irony like a cement block on the place where
the rainbow-hued Soviet confessional poetry of the 1960s used to be.
Khersonsky also mines Brodsky's work for the existential emptiness
and dejection that underlie many of his poems. Most importantly, he
continues Brodsky's reflection on empire as a nauseating phenomenon
that recurs *ad infinitum.*

Yet Khersonsky's purpose is very much his own, and his voice, highly
memorable. His poetry may concur with Brodsky's general, nonconform-
ist, late-Soviet negativism, but it bristles with resistance to empire. The
poem appearing here is an example of his signature tool – parodic double-
voiced discourse – given to a male speaker who cannot imagine himself
apart from the jingoistic, ultra-masculine identity that had been handed
to him by 'warrior ancestors and Lenin's words | and his commandments
and soaring iron birds'. Imperial glory is his only possible glory; ongoing
war, the only way to keep the adrenaline of glory pumping. The speaker
is impotent in any other scenario – so much so as to fantasize about the
murder of his family members; then he could retaliate. Empire and the
idea of the basic human right of life cannot coexist. Khersonsky's parody
pushes the notion of war to its logical conclusion, and provokes rage.

OL

explosions are the new normal...

explosions are the new normal, you grow used to them
stop noticing that you, with your ordinary ways, are a goner
a trigger man and a sapper wander around the park
whispering like a couple – I wish I could eavesdrop

surely, it goes this way: where there's a shovel, there's a tunnel
where there's a conspiracy, there's a catch
where there's God, there's a threshold
stalky Ukrainians – where granny tends to a garden patch

surely it's about the meaning of death, sudden as a mudslide
surely it's about the vodka: to relieve mortal anguish
once you've shown you have any brain, they'll brain you hard into
    submission
hair impeccably parted – where you spot a geometrically neat
    moustache

a trigger man and a sapper wander around like a couple
as the angel of destruction observes them tenderly from the cloud
we're captive birds dear brother that's it that's all
black sun of melancholy shines like a shrapnel hole

OK/PB

modern warfare is too large for the streets...

modern warfare is too large for the streets –
a problem solved by a thousand-pound bomb
its contemporary weight equivalent is sixteen tons
as they sang in the fifties: *goodbye pretty girls*
goodbye company store
we're peaceful people our armoured train stuffed with the spoils of war

we're peaceful people who happen to wear camouflage
three jolly fellows, the combat vehicle crew
broken-off pieces, an industrial collage
I still love my rifle, but a Kalashnikov is a must
the launch of a beautiful friendship in the rocket launcher
hot bullet, hot heart – only the sky is the limit

my beloved rifle, we've reached the end of our shining path
the streets tighten up, you dive into an alley
with all of your battle-ready equipment, your army, your navy
with all of your heart, it doesn't matter that's not the point
he's all muscle, ordinary-looking, possibly an idiot
firemen and militia are looking for him, he's the real hero

safety skills – some twist of the wrist, mind's of no use
stuff a cigarette with gunpowder and the empire goes up in smoke
you cross the boundary, no more boundaries as far as the eye can see
the sky's cloth is tattered and turns into a curtain fringe
black sun rises, a medal on God's chest
now, don't be sad — your life is behind you

OK/PB

when wars are over we just collapse...

when wars are over we just collapse
how do we restore the ruins what to do with the traps
the trenches and useful bunkers and ramparts
where did the damn enemy go the one we dragged
across europe and chased out with our raw force
and where in the world is our victory flag

all full of bullet and shrapnel holes but still victorious
where are the iron sword and the shield of brass
the chainmail and leather quiver filled with arrows
what will we do without all these objects
without our warrior ancestors and Lenin's words
and his commandments and soaring iron birds

when wars are over you don't know what to do anymore
it might even be nice if the enemy knocked on the door
killed your old mother raped your daughter or sister
then we can tighten our belts and stand shoulder to shoulder
march through europe and capture a capital city
and mark this tremendous day in the state calendar

OL/AJ

These poems by Boris Khersonsky are taken from *Words for War: New Poems from Ukraine* (forthcoming from Academic Studies Press, Boston http://www.academicstudiespress.com/forthcoming/wordsforwar Readers of *MPT* will receive a $5 discount on this book by entering the code MPT-WORDS at checkout.

OKSANA LUTSYSHYNA

Translated by the author, Oksana Maksymchuk, Max
Rosochinsky and Olena Jennings

Oksana Lutsyshyna's work draws on the legacy of Ukrainian, Polish,
Russian, and English language writers. The first poem in the selection
('eastern europe is a pit...') reads as a manifesto of a poet oscillating
between two worlds, the old and the new, and two ways of being:
suffering and love. No matter how much she struggles to abandon
her 'Eastern European' perspective, she ends up rolling it back, like
a Sisyphean rock. Eastern Europe has become her own private
nightmare, where time does not move, where the dead poets speak,
where a nervous *parthenos* asks not the question about love, but one
about death.

In the English language, the connotations of 'pit' are infernal,
evoking the 'bottomless pit' of the Bible, with its eternally downward
motion. By contrast, the Ukrainian word *yama* brings to mind a grave:
in such a pit, things are enclosed by the earth, put to rest. One gets
stuck, one cannot move. One cannot even fall, because there's nowhere
to go. Yet this doesn't mean that nothing is happening, for the pit is
seething with its peculiar form of life: things ferment, decompose.
Where there's no motion, there's decay; but decay is itself a form of
being – fresh plums roll down into the pit, new poems emerge.
There's heat here, and energy. As the poet ironically characterizes
her own commitment to the 'national sport' of talking about death,
'sad yet beautiful'. Pains get mixed with pleasures, pleasures get
enhanced by pains.

Lutsyshyna's doctoral dissertation was on Bruno Schulz, a Polish
Jewish writer from Drohobych whose dream-like worlds emerge

from the ceaseless interplay of haughty forms and naughty matter.
Voluptuous things get deflated; small things bubble up, explode.
Lutsyshyna's other poems in the selection are starker, less playful,
yet they too speak of the same themes: *eros* and *thanatos*, determinism
and freedom; of the pit no plum can roll out of, as no plum can stop its
own decay.

OM/MR

eastern europe is a pit of death and decaying plums

eastern europe is a pit of death and decaying plums
I hide from it in the body of america
but sooner or later I'll slip from this light
back down into that other
and will start talking about death because that is our national sport
talking about death
sad yet beautiful
hoping that the world will hear us and gasp at the beauty and sadness

my lover spreads my fingers with his own
he was educated in good old france
then america
he also studied buddhism and erotica somewhere near the borders of
    thailand
it's good to drink wine with him and chat
but not about death or eastern europe
because the world's a shithole and it's worthwhile to learn only one art:

that of hopping from one pleasure islet to another
and not giving a damn about plague-infected continents with their
   corpse-eating flies

he kisses me goodnight and disappears into his dream
as I lie in mine, full of summer sun and ephemeral sweetness
mitteleuropa zbigniew herbert whispers in my ear
middle europe enters a labyrinth without a single turn
a labyrinth of fate and freshly laid brick
it enters and doesn't exit
it endures and revives, small like newly seeded grass in the evening
strong like the grandchildren of those that survived the war
when, when will I die? – someone asks in my still childish voice
but I don't hear the answer because it suddenly becomes dark
in this death pit, where miklos radnoti is writing his last poem

OL/OJ

he asks, don't help me...

he asks, don't help me
help the soldiers
I don't need anything anymore
neither medicine, nor heat, nor light
nor a drink of water

the room I'm leaving is not this one
but the room of my body
they say that God doesn't exist
that the One that exists is human
but as a human – can he exist?
is his existence necessary?

they say that I'm at the end of life
but I still don't understand anything

last night it hurt so bad
that I forgot everything, even who I was
no heaven, no blessed darkness
all I saw were soldiers
I felt their thirst in my bones

don't come to help me
help those who still want to

make children

OM/MR

I Dream of Explosions

someone sets a lighter to a bush of living fire
invisible
with an invisible hand

there's no place on earth that's safe
there's no earth anymore
there's nothing
how can we begin with the words:
'Nothing exists'?

the whole body becomes an organ of sight
finds a foothold
for true vision
you fall out of the world as out of a sieve
and you see: it's not there,
it's an illusion

so why does it still hurt
so bad

OM/MR

These poems by Oksana Lutsyshyna are taken from *Words for War: New Poems from Ukraine* (forthcoming from Academic Studies Press, Boston http://www.academicstudiespress.com/forthcoming/wordsforwar Readers of MPT will receive a $5 discount on this book by entering the code MPT-WORDS at checkout.

VASYL MAKHNO

Translated by Uilleam Blacker

Vasyl Makhno was born in Chortkiv, western Ukraine, in 1964. He left Ukraine in the late 1990s, and, after a short time teaching and writing in Poland, ended up in New York, where he still lives. His early work drew on the rich seams of Ukrainian modernism, in particular on the ecstatic and eclectic genius of the interwar poet Bohdan-Ihor Antonych. His trajectory westwards was accompanied by a move away from modernist forms towards a simpler, more outward-looking sensibility. The poet's eye turned to the strange, new landscapes around him. In New York, he caught the tail end of the activities of the New York Group of post-war Ukrainian émigré poets. His poetry contains fond nods in their direction, but as an immigrant of a different wave, he is more enchanted by New York than his predecessors, and more attuned to its paradoxical mix of local specificity and global reach. Makhno is today surely one of that city's most dedicated poetic chroniclers, flitting between Chinatown markets and Brooklyn bars – watching, listening and recording.

The two poems published here represent a wrenching return eastwards for Makhno. As he spells out in 'War Generation': 'you may live in New York but you are always | a soldier of your unit – your country – its troubles'. Even a drifter cannot help but be drawn homeward when his home is under threat. The poems are urgent, direct, and violent, in a manner uncharacteristic for Makhno. But perhaps the most effective is 'On Apollinaire', where the poet glances back at his earlier, modernist repertoire of dense imagery and symbolism, yet without losing sight of the gravity of the subject: the exhaustion and devastation of an unexpected war.

War Generation

each generation must fight its own war
each in that generation bears his own guilt
you may live in New York but you are always
a soldier of your unit – your country – its troubles

you're a soldier of the air – its commando
your country's army is a flying garden
shielding the heavens, the source that feeds
the earth beneath your feet, its simple seed

your sole defence is your heart – and a flak jacket
today you must forget that you are a poet
you must come here and stand – there's room in the ranks
merge into the Dnipro – its protective banks

your standard-issue boots squeeze your feet
your unit digs trenches – and digs in its heels
each one's a soldier in this earth-seed generation
each one is capable of carrying a machine gun

war will come for each generation
filled up with light – but still more with scum
with the dirty boots of funeral guards
with mourning marches and army ballads

On Apollinaire

while we may call snow a flute – which among all the flutes
of language is the finest stem – the deepest well to hide
sounds, the fanfares of interwar silence, so beloved of the lieu-
tenant: who tells his soldiers to study the military trade

snow in the business of war is no fault of flutes or fanfares
a plane flies like an angel through the heavens, scattering the feathers
of the hawk's victim wrapped in white, like a cut-out sheet of darkness
nervously sealing the holes in the flute's ragged corpse

perhaps in that music between silver and bronze – all snow and water –
it rises like a sail, like a ship's pitch-covered bottom –
the lieutenant forgets orders and hallucinates: the almonds will flower
and the soldiers melt like snow through the village, seeking port wine

lucid in his dreams, he bleeds from his head – Apollinaire
has forgotten something – in the end he'll ask for pickled cabbage juice,
but there are no villagers here, the angel of death arrives, opens the door
shuts his eyes, wraps him in music, and then cuts loose

his boat on the river, the soldiers bring wine, sit downcast on the hilltop,
make a tent from their rifles and pull dried bread from their pockets
washing it down with their wine, sadness and surrealism –
death is here – all around them lurk ravens and foxes

These poems by Vasyl Makhno are taken from *Words for War: New Poems
from Ukraine* (forthcoming from Academic Studies Press, Boston
http://www.academicstudiespress.com/forthcoming/wordsforwar
Readers of *MPT* will receive a $5 discount on this book by entering the
code MPT-WORDS at checkout.

OSTAP SLYVYNSKY

Translated by Anton Tenser and Tatiana Filimonova

Slyvynsky is a masterful DJ. The storybook structure of his narratives teems with unmistakable realia of contemporary everyday life. Third person narratives, as if clandestinely overheard by the reader and author simultaneously, represent small cross-sections in time that betray a knowledge of larger, possibly catastrophic events that remain outside of our field of vision. Slyvynsky's power lies in making us believe that these larger, four-dimensional stories really exist beyond the synchronic slice of the poem's text; that a poem's centre of gravity is to be found outside its body.

Lovers on a Bicycle

She rides sitting on the frame, like a bird
perched on a branch, puffed-up, mature,
with two clenched
knees that signal sweetly
to the truck drivers passing by.

Him we don't see clearly, but we hear
his flask clanking against the seat with every
pedal stroke. He's humming a ditty,
where did he pick it up, which war zone? No one's heard it here.

She holds a handful of hazelnuts and feeds him
without turning – she passes them back and he
catches them with his mouth, which resembles
a fringed brown patch.

On the way back from the station she'll be alone,
looking like a paper doll,
dry, straight, two-dimensional,
used to making do with this love, as she
is used to making a meal out of nothing –
a dash of tea, a couple of potatoes.
She will ride through the first bout of rain,
reeling with her feet the over-exposed film – an endless
blank frame, where he runs into the living room
and spins her in his arms.

So it goes, this empty language of love, bargaining with hope,
like a one-legged chair with a stove: let me be
at least until midday. I won't
live through the night.

Latifa

'The kid asks, of course... He asks
when we will head back home.
And so one time I told him. I said: our house
was taken up to the sky. I don't know
what I was thinking. I said:
our house was so good to us, Alim,
that it could not stand on earth anymore
like all other houses.
And it had so much love,
so many layers of love
we applied to the floor, the doors,
the window panes,
and as soon as the old love peeled off,
we would put on a new layer, even more diligently
and generously; ever brighter white and red
was the love we put on. Also, ivory-coloured
love, although grandpa said that's not real love,
just childish games. Because for love
a simple colour should be enough.
All of this I say to myself, and to the kid
I say: yes, you could see nothing but
the sky from the windows now.
And angels, too.
But there is no one home.
Because angels are not for the living to see.'

Orpheus

But really this whole story
has a backstory, and it is about
a kid who was afraid of water.
But he would still go with everyone to the beach and clamber up
the long rock,
and when the boys jumped into the sea, he stayed behind,
standing there, skinny and lost,
and watched them grow distant,
their heads in ruffles of splashes,
with the single hope
that none of them look back.
And then he would head for the nearby
buildings, slashing thistle heads, helpless,
different from everyone else here
resembling a copper string, accidentally
weaved into a basket.
You know this kid?
You know at what point
music comes out of anger, like a butterfly
emerging out of a frostbitten cocoon?
You know where he was until morning, when
his parents found him in the grass, sweaty,
with clenched teeth?
And tell me this: how much anger can a poem hold?
Just enough to
drown out the sirens?

A Scene From 2014

'For years I would wake up
when he returned from his night shift, around three or four
in the morning. He showered for a long time
and went to bed just as black, coal-like,
almost invisible
in the dark. Did he simply dissolve one night?'
                    We're silent.
In a moment she bursts into laughter: some kid
runs past us, trips
and falls – right on top of the flour sack that
he's carrying,
                    and his sneakers fly up high
in the heart of a little white cloud –
                    so white, this explosion,
she says, so quiet.

These poems by Ostap Slyvynsky are taken from *Words for War: New Poems from Ukraine* (forthcoming from Academic Studies Press, Boston http://www.academicstudiespress.com/forthcoming/wordsforwar Readers of MPT will receive a $5 discount on this book by entering the code MPT-WORDS at checkout.

SERHIY ZHADAN

Translated by Amelia Glaser, Yuliya Ilchuk and Ilya Kaminsky

Serhiy Zhadan, an internationally acclaimed poet and novelist – oh, and front-man for the popular ska-band 'Dogs in Space' – has put his art to the service of Ukraine's war-torn Donbas border region. Born in 1974, Zhadan studied and taught Ukrainian and world literature at the University of Kharkiv until his 'retirement' from teaching in 2004 to focus solely on his writing. The author of over a dozen collections of poetry, five novels, and several collections of short stories, Zhadan, whose first books of poetry appeared in the 1990s, has more recently become known as a civic poet and public intellectual committed to developing an inclusive society in Ukraine. A native of Eastern Ukraine, Serhiy Zhadan was active in the Kharkiv protests in 2014 and was badly beaten while peacefully demonstrating. He has since worked to provide humanitarian aid and works towards peace in the zone of military conflict, co-founding, in February 2017, the Serhiy Zhadan Charitable Foundation, which assists communities in the Donbas. In his collections published since the war broke out (*Life of Maria* (2015) and *Tamplers* (2016)) the poet presents the conflict in a series of meditations with hints of the religious in both content and form. In Zhadan's vision, Ukraine, like many other countries in Europe, has entered its own version of the Middle Ages, i.e. a long-lasting war for an idea that consumes those on both sides of the front-line.

Zhadan's recent cycles of poetry incorporate conversations with individuals the poet has met in Donbas, but some of these types, the Protestant missionary, the hardened 'bro', the drunk, will be familiar to readers of his pre-War works. Zhadan's poetry is at once specific to Eastern Ukraine and highly translatable. His line is spare – avoiding

Serhiy Zhadan © Valentyn Kuzan

excess pathos and striking a balance between the serious and the sentimental. 'Headphones' channels Sasha – a lonely figure navigating a lonelier world, a figure who, in spite of it all, manages to preserve humanity and even art. 'Rhinoceros' compares the exotic concept of death to an exotic animal at the zoo. The title suggests the characters from Ionescu's *Rhinoceros* who, falling prey to the reigning ideology, become wild beasts. Zhadan has an ear for the colloquial and the rhythmic. The candid, factual lines that open 'Needle' yield to the more sensuous repetition of 'B'esh, b'esh, tatuiuval'niku' (Carve, carve, tattoo-artist). Zhadan will sacrifice slang and romance alike for hard-hitting truth. In 'Needle', the tattoo artist who 'exists to fill the world with meaning' is taken out in the most meaningless of places – at a roadblock. But the final lines of the poem deliver the harshest blow. Is this, the Donbas war, the stuff of heroic poems? Perhaps. Or perhaps, instead, the incident will be forgotten. That is to say, this poem, without ever calling the events in Donbas a 'war', is also a poem about what war means, and about how individuals living through war or peace, leave their marks on the world.

AG/YI

From 'Why I am not on Social Media'

Needle

Anton, age thirty-two.
Status: 'living with parents'.
Orthodox, but didn't go to church,
finished college, took English as his foreign language.
Worked as a tattoo artist, had a signature style,
if you can call it that.
Lots of folks from our local crowd passed through
his skilful hands and sharp needle.
When all this started, he talked a lot about
politics and history, started going to rallies,
fell out with friends.
Friends took offence, clients disappeared.
People got scared, didn't get it, left town.
You feel a person best when you touch her with a needle.
A needle stings, a needle stitches. Beneath
its metallic warmth the texture of a woman's skin is so supple,
the bright canvas of male skin's so stiff.
Piercing that outer shell,
you release the body's velvet beads
of blood. Carve, carve out
angels' wings on the submissive surface of the world.
Carve, carve, tattoo artist, for our calling
is to fill this world with meaning, to fill it
with colours. Carve, tattoo artist, this
outer lining, which hides souls and diseases –
all that we live for, all that we will die for.
Someone said they shot him at a roadblock,

in the morning, a weapon in his hands, somehow by accident –
No one knew what happened.
They buried him in a mass grave (they buried them all that way).
His possessions were returned to his parents.
Nobody updated his status.
There will come a time when some bastard
will surely write heroic poems about this.
There will come a time when some other bastard
will say this isn't worth writing about.

AG/YI

Headphones

Sasha, a quiet alcoholic, esoteric, poet,
spent the whole summer in the city.
Surprised when the shelling started,
he turned on the news, then quit watching.
He roams the city, never removing his headphones,
listening to dinosaurs,
he runs into burnt-out cars,
and dismembered bodies.

All of history,
the world where we once lived,
has left us the words and music of a few geniuses
who tried, and failed, to warn us,
tried to explain something or other,

but explained nothing, saved no one.
In graveyards,
their genius rib cages
sprout flowers and grass.
Nothing else will be left –
just the music, just the words, just a voice
forcing us to love.

You never have to turn this music off.
Listen to outer space, your eyes shut tight.
Think about whales in the night ocean.
There's nothing else to hear.
Nothing else to see.
Nothing else to feel.
Except the smell, of course.
Except the smell of corpses.

AG/YI

Rhinoceros

Half a year she's held firm.
Half a year she's observed death
the way you observe a rhinoceros at the zoo –
dark folds,
heavy breathing.
She's scared, but doesn't look away,
doesn't close her eyes.

It's terrifying, really terrifying.
And it should be.
Death is terrifying, it frightens.
It's terrifying to smell the stink of a blood moon.
It's terrifying to see how history is made.

Half a year ago everything was completely different.
Half a year ago everyone was different.
No one got scared
when stars fell over the reservoir.
No one startled when smoke
rose from cracks in the black earth.

In the middle of the night street,
in the middle of the clamour and headlights,
in the middle of death and love
she buries her face in his shoulder,
pounds him desperately with her fists,
weeps, screams in the dark.
I don't, she says, want to see all this.
I can't carry all this inside me.
What do I need so much death for?
What am I supposed to do with it?

What can you do with death?
Carry it on your back,
like a Gypsy child –
Nobody loves him,
and he loves no one.
There is so little love,
love is so defenceless.

Cry and shatter the dark with your warm hands.
Cry and don't step away.
The world will never be the way it was before.
We'll never let it
be the way it was before.

Ever fewer lighted windows on the cold street.
Ever fewer carefree passers-by
around the shop windows.
In the hellish autumn dusk, fields and rivers cool.
The bonfires go out in the rain.
The cities grow numb at night.

AG/YI

The Street. A Woman Zigzags The Street

The street. A woman zigzags the street.
A pause. By the grocery
she hesitates.
Shall she buy bread, there is not – is there enough? – not enough bread
    at home.
Shall she buy bread now, or – tomorrow? – she considers.
Stares at. Stares at her phone. Rings. Rings.

Speaks to mother: Mother.
Speaks abruptly, without listening
she shouts.
Shouts

by the store window; at the store window,
as if she is shouting at herself in the store window.
Slaps the phone.
Zigzags the street, cursing
her invisible – and therefore even more
cursed – mother.

Tears. Tears of pain at her
mother
and at the impossibility of forgiving
her mother. Forget
the bread.
Forget it. Forget the bread and everything else on this earth. Forget it.
    Forgo it. Leave it alone.

That morning
it begins. The first aerial bombardment.

IK

These poems by Serhiy Zhadan are taken from *Words for War: New Poems from Ukraine* (forthcoming from Academic Studies Press, Boston http://www.academicstudiespress.com/forthcoming/wordsforwar Readers of *MPT* will receive a $5 discount on this book by entering the code MPT-WORDS at checkout.

IRYNA SHUVALOVA

Translated by the author

Finding a way to speak about war, the tremendous toll it takes and the pain it inflicts is always a great challenge for a poet. For me, as a writer, reader and translator of poetry, there are two things that work best in war writing, making it at least somewhat adequate to its gargantuan task. One is extreme down-to-earth precision, the chronicling of the minute details of war, of the small cogs of its horrible machinery churning out death. The other one, on the opposite side of the spectrum, is the writing of the universal mythology of war, its anatomizing as a shared human experience, a terrible heritage of our pride and greed, an echo of pain in our chromosomes. War writing at its best, I think, is both: the particular and the universal tightly wound together. And although I can only hope to achieve this perfect balance, I do always remember that whether we want it or not, we are all history, and history unavoidably harkens back to myth (or is it the other way round?). Hence, we are all the mythical creatures and the stuff of legends. This is precisely how I write everything and everyone in my poems, including myself: no matter whether in love or war.

our dead

our dead
always reply to us
with silence

their mouths
are like dry riverbeds
black sand is dropping from under their eyelashes
rust is eating up their ancient sorrows

our dead
always reply
with silence

they chew on their own
                   long
                        footsteps
they wave goodbye from under the water
to our passing boats

from our plates
they pick the breadcrumbs of our shame

their long roots
reach deep
into our families and genera

our dead remain silent
              reclining
the rivers of sand run between their vertebrae

their clenched teeth
crush the iron cords
of the fresh
    green
       grass

our dead toll
like big bronze bells
endless trains of rain passing through their veins

their place
is in the womb
of the earth
amidst the blind stones and convulsing roots

our dead
grow
they become
taller than us

they
carry our time in handfuls

never making it through
always spilling it

in the dust

into the sweet orchard

you will go, woman, into the sweet orchard
a bone through a throat
a chunk of clay that melts
slowly burying yourself
in the dark pond of his body

you'll go as if into a river
first – a large fish
with a white stomach full of dreams
second – a bloody berry
a closed fist full of bitter seeds
third – an empty jar
with a narrow neck full of song

each time you enter you won't have a name
each time you enter you'll carry a mouthful of names
you'll swallow them beyond the gates
so that again you won't have any
so that you can return

love fish

the love fish
lives in the large body of the river
it swims in it like a pendulum
back and forth and in a circle
fastened to the heart's axis

it patiently meanders
from the water's roots
to its spreading branches
swims paths that are covered
with only your traces

the love fish sings
with a frog's mouth
with an ant's voice
oh how ugly it is how blind
not worth the slightest mention in the thinnest book

so hungry
that it eats shadows
touches, traces of kisses
on the warm throat of the day

it knows that out of all names
your name is the dearest
and so
swimming into the deep wells
it sheds large round stone tears

falling heavily to the bottom
through the thick clear water

the love fish
knows
that your name rings
like bracelets on the wrists
of a gypsy dancer
that it echoes like
a bag of copper coins scattered
in a large empty church
or like the sound of soldiers in the square
throwing down their weapons all at once
a thousand swords

your name is sharp
when taken tenderly beneath the tongue
it pierces the mouth
and the tip
comes through the lip

swim love fish
while your big tree of water grows
while the iron hook in your lip
lives its quiet life

keeping you tethered
and tenderly pulling
ever closer to

home

LIDA YUSUPOVA

Translated by Ainsley Morse and Bela Shayevich

The poet and prose writer Lida Yusupova was born in the Soviet
Union, in Petrozadovsk, a small city that in Soviet times was both
ordinarily provincial and unusually open to the West – and even to
Outer Space. But, alas, she slept through the famous 1977 alien
visitation. After being forced to abandon her studies at Leningrad
State University, Yusupova worked at the post office. When she hung a
portrait of Isaac Babel over her cot in the dormitory, the other post
girls thought it was her father. Her first book, *Irasaliml'*, came out in
1995. In 1996 Yusupova left Russia, first for Jerusalem, then Toronto,
and in 2004 Yusupova moved to Belize.

Yusupova's poetry presents a strong documentary impulse in
combination with a striking intimacy, an approach profoundly
appropriate to the violence – often sexual violence – that lurks beneath
and suddenly rises to the surface of many of her poems. The official
wordage of reports and legal documents can sometimes contradict the
lyric speaker, even drowning her out – but she is also capable of
pronouncing and manipulating this alienating language herself. The
resulting discursive tension charges Yusupova's work with great
dramatic power. It also underscores the mutability of her lyric
speakers, who not only appropriate the language of the state, but
also embody radical empathy toward individual perpetrators of
violence. In Yusupova's poems, these individuals are never merely
self-contained, externalized signifiers of evil; just as she does with
bureaucratic language, Yusupova occupies the evil from within,
looking out through the murderer's 'beautiful eyes' (the title of a
poem from *Dead Dad*). Non-violent death, as in the memorial poems
in Yusupova's most recent collection, *Dead Dad*, is also subjected to
unsettling emotional interrogation from a perspective at once
shockingly intimate and distanced.

Dead Dad

I

the dad's body
on the floor
in detail, down to the tiniest hair
not sleeping no
indisputably dead
but born of the imagination
not like in Lucien Freud
the mother's contorted mouth
here we have thin calm lips

when he's not there he's closer
I couldn't say
close
but closer
when he was alive he was not there at all

the dick of Ron Mueck's dead dad shows
        4 o'clock
I saw my dad's dick once
'papa, what time is it?'
'th f!'

mama calls and says
papa died at 4 a.m. ay ay die
(actually no one called me
        I found out about my dad's death almost
        twenty-four hours later - by email)

I don't know what time he died
the only one who knows is some nurse
who doesn't remember it, she just goes on living
            with that date in her brain

Ron Mueck gave dead dad his hair

it looks like one of the Chernobyl spiderwebs
I read about in the *New York Times* yesterday

my hair came from my dad

Chernobyl spiders weave jazzy
            webs

Ron Mueck gave dead dad his hair
my dead dad gave me my hair

I never saw my dad alive just like
 I don't see myself

I needed more time
            to get to the body
            of my dad
than my mother did to hide him
in the ground
in a mountain

Ron Mueck made the silicone body
            of his dead dad
remembering his dad alive

his dad turned out quite small
only 90 cm long

...

the one who's close is further away for me
and the ones further away are the opposite

which means the people I can't understand the most
(like Peter Woodcock)
are dearer to me than everyone else

my life with my father consisted of
            idiotic fragments
throwaways
except for one
when he kissed me
everyone kissed me and he kissed me too
(giggling nervously)
it was the first time his face got that close
pink cheeks
suddenly childlike
(grandma used to dress him up as a girl
a little blonde angel
everyone would say
what a pretty little girl)
at the Petrozavodsk city hospital
in 1995
when everyone thought I was dying

and he kissed me goodbye
a little girl angel
giggling
girl superhero
on the spire of the empire state building
at least for that one second
and it could have never happened at all

2
Kenny Bennett, who I love a lot,
wrote an essay called 'Why I started going
        to school'

I don't know why you want to know
        why I went to school
but since you want to know so much
or more like since you decided to ask me
        this question
the answer to which
be honest with yourselves, people
doesn't interest you at all
fine

here's why I started going to school
again
when I turned 20

I went back to school because my dad
was showing me the stars above Dangriga
at night on the roof
and was teaching me to smoke pot
nobody anywhere has as many stars as in Dangriga
and when I was sad sometimes anyway
and I would go into the jungle to be
          by myself there
my dad would dress up as Tata Duende
a little man with a wide-brimmed
          hat
a child abductor
dad would squat down and put his boots on
          facing backwards
wrap himself in a trench coat
and jump on me out of the dark
so that I would understand how dangerous it was to go out
          alone at night
dad taught me how to love women
we'd hire them together at the bar
my dad and I would get into fistfights
not with each other
we'd get drunk and fight people
          who deserved to get beat up
we'd run from the cops together
my dad taught me how to run fast

when my son died
dad cried on the phone
and said that Rosa was the one who killed him

my son had Down's syndrome
plus asthma
he was only 4 when he died
at night
he was all alone
his mother, Rosa, was in the next room
          with her boyfriend
I didn't want to see his dead body
I didn't go to the funeral
I will never forgive Rosa

my five other children are alive and well

I want to study the stars
like Arlie Petters
you know he's from Dangriga too
because nobody anywhere has stars
          like the ones in Dangriga

my mum smokes crack and now she's had
          a stroke
I can't forget her number
I've forgotten every other phone number
I don't even remember my little brother's number
but I can't forget hers
but I don't want to call her
and I don't even have a phone

why did I go back to school
I went back to school so my dad would be happy

so that he would be happy
I went to school to make my dad
        happy
even if he's dead

Kenny Bennett, San Pedro College
San Pedro, Belize

Funkspiel

mama was laying wallpaper
I was sitting on the floor watching her
she turned sharply:
what're you gaping at?
this was all observed by aliens
who noted:
here we have a little girl crying
blue wallpaper with silvery flowers Lake Shapshozero lies 198 metres
from the dacha building
August 28 1942 four pilots of two sh-twos shot themselves in the lake
Piotr Alekseevich Chaikin (by other sources Chaika)
Piotr Naumovich Shulga
Pavel Nikolaevich Andreev
Andrei Ivanovich Mogut (by other sources Feodor Motuz)
reaped in the funkspiel
maybe we should start a funkspiel with this little girl
and see how she does
when we open nonexistent doors for her
initiate her into impossible mysteries
bring her in contact with the dead men
in the sludgy lake with its swans

my grandpa was made of soap

my grandpa was made of soap
and wrote books about uprisings
he'd give me wind-up bears
each bear had a little key in its back
if you turned the key
the bear'd come alive
and slowly blankly turn circles
our gazes never met
once in winter
I found grandpa's letter to my dad
sent to Yakutia
where dad was washing gold
it was a didactic letter
consisting of platitudes
it was written in the lovely handwriting
of grandpa's ichthyologist wife
it swims against the current down the dark
        hallway
and looks at me
looks

ELENA KOSTYLEVA

Translated by Helena Kernan

This is a poem from a recent cycle written and performed by
Russian poet Elena Kostyleva at a spoken word event at the bookshop
Poryadok Slov in St. Petersburg in August. Her work is fiercely
politically engaged, rooted in the female experience and utterly
arresting to listen to, thanks to its intricate sound play.

Written in the aftermath of the revelations of the torture and
execution of gay men in Chechnya earlier this year, the poem is a visual
and aural onslaught, an expression of outrage at human rights abuses
taking place in the poet's own country. Based on conversations with a
real person living in Chechnya, the poem unfolds like a mantra or a
fugue, suffused with sexual imagery and patterns of hard, brutal
consonants. The introductory passage is the poet's attempt to make
sense of the current literary vogue for writing about violence in its
many forms and mocks superficial efforts to shock and disturb. Her
discussion of the ethics of representation provides a critical lens for
viewing the poetry that follows: how can atrocities be recorded without
being glorified or somehow wounding the listener? The poem itself
will be published in Russian for the first time this autumn in the
journal *Sled*.

The poem makes allusion to a group on Vkontakte, the most
popular Russian social network, called 'Why are the mountains
silent?'. It acts as a forum allowing LGBT people in the Caucasus to
communicate and make contact with each other.

◆

'So what kind of violence are you interested in?' I ask Lyuba
Makarevskaya, editor of the journal *Sled*. 'Gender-based? Imaginary?
Real? The kind happening in Syria? Patriarchal? Do you have to pose
as a victim of some sort of violence in order to write for fashionable
journals? Little girls pissed on someone at nursery – does that count?
Or what about watching 3D monster porn? Isn't that a bit anti-
monster? Literature is supposed to ask incisive questions.

'In any case, doesn't all writing about violence implicitly delight
in it? Surely at the very least it shouldn't be figurative. It shouldn't
describe or picture violence. Poetry is the freest art, and it rejected
representation a long time ago. Nowadays, visual artists are also
abandoning it: photography and video aren't narrative tools any
more. It started with the rejection of painting – a rejection of the
violence that painting does to the artist.'

◆

I WANT ONLY YOU AND THE TORTURE OF GAYS
ONLY YOU, CHECHNYA
ONLY HARDCORE
MOUNTAINS SWORN
TO SILENCE
AND YOU, CHECHNYA

IF THEY FIND OUT THEY'LL SHOOT YOU
ONLY YOU, CHECHNYA
I'M SENDING YOU SOMETHING
ON CHAT, IF THEY FIND IT
THEY'LL SHOOT
BEHIND THE WOODEN SHACK
NOT PENETRATING
OR OPENING YOU UP, CHECHNYA

I'M PUTTING SOMETHING IN MY MOUTH
SOMETHING THAT'S YOURS, CHECHNYA
ONLY
YOURS,
CHECHNYA

CHAT
ONLY CHECHNYA
CHAT
CHECHNYA

THAT'S IT

HELGA OLSHVANG

Translated by Ainsley Morse

With her Scandinavian name and elegant, cosmopolitan sensibility, Helga Olshvang can be hard to place – and 'Russian poet' is indeed only one of her many callings, which include filmmaker, mother and screenwriter (she also works under the name Helga Landauer). The first poem I translated for her involved a complicated metaphor combining fish scales and montage, and the cinematic orientation is evident throughout the poems of her most recent collection (from which this selection was made): an exquisite shot, the right light, the long take during which the speaker cannot look away, no matter how much she ducks and deflects. But Olshvang is simultaneously a full-blown Russian poet in the refined Russian Modernist tradition, evoking Boris Pasternak in her attention to everyday objects infused with emotional intensity, and Anna Akhmatova – incidentally the subject of one of her films – in her subtle but profound evocation of the experience of being a woman.

Translating Olshvang is no simple task – the poems here were selected in part for their greater translatability, but there is no escaping the intricate interlingual play that runs through Olshvang's work. My sense as a translator was that years of living in English have sharpened this poet's attention to the grammatical and morphological peculiarities (read poetic possibilities) of her native tongue. The proximity to English also inspires poetic experimentation. The title of this latest collection, taken from one of the poems, is a fine example of this: *Blue is White [Goluboe eto beloe]*. These three words convey a great deal of Olshvang's poetic approach: the observation that the English 'blue' sounds closer to the Russian word 'white' (*beloe*) turns into a statement that only makes concrete sense in the space between these languages (the Russian title, in a vacuum, is just as mysterious at first glance as is the English). In the poem ('with its consonants and

non-consenters...') I translated it as 'blue is *beloe*', a decision that
doesn't really solve the problem but at least reveals its interlingual
nature. I should also give credit here to Olshvang herself, who worked
with me on these translations.

Can't See Where We Are...

Can't see where we are, who you are – can't see.
An alternating current
squeezes the inward sides of the body, the walls, the mainlines,
but now we're the ones who use legs and feet and tongues and backs
to make a beast,
we knew it would come to be this dark.
When out of the sleeves, the hats,
the bottlenecks, the boots and folds
comes tumbling, naked,
weeping toward the world – a mortal,
dawning and smelling of rubbing alcohol
this world, clanking in time
to the shudders and body's attempts to fall
into body, when the light
suddenly, with a click,
burns out, an occasion for life –
find it, consciousness, itself. Look,
here it is – the beast
in question.

Logs

Water of the spruce's under sun
grey bark,
under wind.
Torn all at once
the whole sky from the water – such, time,
is your surface.
Adhesive base.
The crackle of water. The bark
of shining pines, boulders, crows.

A Fish Plunged, a Man Died...

A fish plunged, a man died.
The needle the tack
steering down.
From inside-out and above
non-being a seam stretched –
– a burn
along the birthing mother's belly and a whistle
on the exhale – on the inh...
faltering. Out of
you what was dragged out by the gills in passing
will rise again – alive.
Will go on apart.

with its consonants and non-consenters...

with its consonants and non-consenters speech goes off the rails,
called
to a strange land to speak
in hard words
words'
skins
cover sense
I speak out what needs to be said
I hold out *love me not*
a plea
language links and catches
the earlier I
looked like *you*
in English
a fallen word
speak of the devil and fall
out of your mind
blue is *beloe*
wavering white

O, I...

O, I,
who know no words and all
amok, the time to say it has come, I,
listen: who we are, who appear to be one,
to the ones looking back askance, hero to hero.

I like any other,
taking myself by the elbows,
I do a little dance, here I take the subway
and take water into my mouth – a pledge
of a word so unspeakable – I go mute.

I, whose hiding place to track from –
you won't keep up, knee to knee,
hair to hair, spitting image of a pomegranate
inserting itself inside – wound into wound,

to a T like how the tongue, and sounds, roared
in glossolalia, I, out from the hitch bar
they danced the word into the crack.
To say that out loud – didn't work.

No bird flutters from the breast,
no gesture,
o, and not your own tail, not even a rose
the sound of being – it was, it was not, – the bridge
curving back.

ALINA DADAEVA

Translated by Josephine von Zitzewitz

My first taste of Dadaeva's writing was a single poem, 'Perevernutyi mir khrupok' (Upside down the world is brittle), published in the journal *Zvezda* in 2010. I soon sought out more of her poetry and was sad to learn that the author has switched to writing mostly prose over the last couple of years.

Dadaeva is an acute observer of everyday details as well as of her inner world. Her poetic musings are deliberate, slow and intriguing. At the same time, sound takes primacy over discursive meaning, driving the poem forward and creating a web of new allusions that can pose a challenge to the translator. Another characteristic feature is the scarcity of verbs in her lines – it is perfectly possible in Russian to have sentences without finite verbs, unlike in English. This means that the translator often has to substitute verbs, possibly adding new nuances of meaning in the process.

Dust on the Ottoman Divan...

Dust on the ottoman divan,
on your plate
salted dried apricots.
Sleep-heavy donkeys
cradle sun between their ears,
a rickety cloud's
awkward smiley
shows a bitter grin.
In your throat
a deflated ball,
a balloon,
take a breath and fly wherever you want.
The shutters tick
or perhaps it's the crickets.
The gutter
is blocked
by a rock
lying across it,
dash-like.

The Soul is Resilient in Her Own Way...

The soul is resilient in her own way,
has her own fortress of Brest-Litovsk
Half-ruined,
a single blind window
Looking out on the heath.

Walls
        oppress me,
        they don't order me
To tremble in the wind like an aspen leaf,
Covered in cracks all over,
goose flesh.

What a shame that this place is public,
Rhymes
        are the same old paparazzi,
When I leave
I'll put up a sign
'under restoration'.

KSENIYA ZHELUDOVA

Translated by Josephine von Zitzewitz

I was searching for new Russian poets I might enjoy reading when I picked up Kseniya Zheludova's first collection, *Slovno*. These poems, written between 2009 and 2013, struck me in their immediacy and the unflinching honesty of the emotions expressed. But above all, I was taken by Zheludova's voice, which is not only fresh, but fully-formed and unmistakable.

Her poems are formally intriguing, written in a free metre held together by strong end rhymes. In this they resemble the work of Elena Shvarts, a prominent St Petersburg poet who died in 2010.

But while St Petersburg sometimes forms the backdrop to Zheludova's poems, the city is rarely the focus. Instead, it fuses with the internal landscapes she draws with only a few words. These landscapes use the markers of the outside world – a harbour, the bottom of the sea, kitchen shelves – to render everyday emotions and situations visible, palpable: despair, love for life, conflicted relationships. Her seemingly conversational tone masks the fact that these poems are tightly wrought lyrical creations. The way Zheludova makes her language work means that her often stark, confident assertions assume an irrefutable logic when sound associations suggest or reinforce new causal connections. While it has been impossible to retain the original rhyme schemes in my translations, I have tried to intimate the central quality of Zheludova's poetry – language-driven, with bold conclusions the reader finds impossible to resist.

Memo

read, learn this by heart:
there's a limit to darkness, all sadness
can be overcome, just build a bridge;
pain is exhaustible, sorrow not bottomless,
if you dare to stand tall
and stretch after happiness, since it's
within your reach, and its recipe utterly simple.

write it down, then burn the sheet later:
people are concentric circles
around the very same heart.
memory is a tiny nail hammered into your head,
if you learn to forgive, half of it will come out.
injuries and grief ripen into a taut bunch,
squeeze out the last drop, you'll get bitter wine.

grow up, but don't even think of growing old,
death exists, but that's all it is
– death,
tribute to the law of contrast.
numbering the pages is a waste of effort
since time's beyond your control.
what you can do is remember words, names and
faces,
tear down walls, hold borders in contempt
love until your heart smoulders

and know that none of it is in vain.

Words

words go away then come back, turn full circle;
or it's you who stays faithful to words, crazy from lack of language;
in any case, we need to talk, my friend.
for example, let's talk about how
an artist or juggler loses their hands,
how a submarine sinks to the sea's marshy bottom
while the commander does a headcount of his boys,
gulping air with his mouth open.

...he says: I can defend you, I can deal with any misfortune
I am so strong, I'll put paid to all your troubles at once,
fear nothing;
then he buys himself a huge house
on an elm tree street

...eliza comes to a city of mast-like pines and ship masts,
of white nights and bedtime stories – the storyteller drinking beer
    and honey,
a city of brazen wind she accepts in place of lovers,
and their comforting lullabies,
of cemeteries where she weaves shirts
from stinging nettles

... she hears someone mouthing 'I love you', looks outside, eyes sad,
she should have said 'I don't love you' and once and for all stayed on
    this side of the abyss,
instead she says 'you're very nice, but',

turning an act of awkwardness into
one of recklessness

...eliza leaves the city where the rain's mixed of Neva river water and
    cheap vodka,
where the Hermitage's cold corner stands out from the mist,
inside, an invigilator fell asleep on a bent-wood chair;
a storm warning,
three wise men in a frail, hole-ridden boat
sailed out onto the Gulf, had a think and drowned...

... and when the radio announces, triumphantly, that war has begun,
he says: turn it off, they won't give us any truth from now;
later he listens closely and says:
think of it, really, a torn string.
oh lord, how empty and joyful,
oh lord, how cheerless.

The Only Real Thing We Have is the Past...

The only real thing we have is the past:
the present's not really present,
the future is nothing to count on
seems we're standing on the central square,
around us people rage and bustle,
hang around, potter about,
exhausted;
not really beggars,
not hopeless,
but haggard inside,
barely dragging their legs,
downright shadows
dried up,
dead.

behind the central square there are knights on the bridge,
I'll go and stand next to them on the highest chair,
they've been dreaming of their last battle for centuries
I'll stand here, awaiting my own

TIMUR KIBIROV

Translated by James Womack

Political poems, but it is difficult to think of Timur Kibirov as primarily a political poet. For one thing, it is hard to know exactly which direction he is coming from: his reflexes are so ironic, his ear for the falseness of public language is so acute, and his high-spirited desire to play with that falseness is so difficult to tame that every statement he makes ends up embodying or at least gesturing at its opposite. There is a tradition in modern Russian writing called *stiob*: parody which hews so closely to what it is parodying that it is difficult to catch; a form of writing that is the verbal equivalent of a glance or a half-caught wink. You see it in the inherent difficulty in parsing the aims and insistences of these poems: the future may be dead, as Kibirov's reworking of Hans Christian Andersen suggests, but the past isn't looking all that happy either. The answer, of course, is to realize that you are asking the wrong questions, are stuck between the wrong poles. Tradition is not the answer, but neither is it the enemy; the standard Russian faith in the power of literature as a balance to the state is overrated, but still present. So, for example, the poem 'Historiosophical' takes up, and riffs on, the most famous of all Russian self-definitions, Tiutchev's clichéd stanza *Umom Rossiyu ne ponyat'*, but puts it in a liminal, perhaps ironic, perhaps entirely devout, new context. These are clear-eyed and surprisingly strong poems that deliberately aim to throw us off balance.

Hurriedly, in Premature Celebration...

The roses bloom! Oh this is Paradise!
And we shall see the infant Christ!
– Andersen, 'The Snow Queen'

1
Hurriedly, in premature celebration,
the little boy bursts again from the crowd
and says, once more: 'But the king isn't wearing...'

then he clams up,
as he sees
that not only the king,
but all his retinue
(the ministers, Life Guards, ladies-in-waiting,
even the two con-men tailors themselves...)

are all naked!
All of them literally
in their birthday suits!

He spins in confusion
back to the gathered crowd
and beholds only naked bodies,
the denuded
woeful flesh of humanity.

And now, confused and fearful,
he senses his own naked,

goose-fleshed, bluish,
little boy's skin,

and sees leafless trees in the distance,
sees how the forest has been stripped,
how the fields are bare,
how the naked earth is a desert

and winter is on its way...

Now who, who will wrap us up warm,
us, who have been stripped of everything?
Who, who will protect us,
the little naked soldiers
of a naked king?

2

For our leader is bare,
and his queen is the snow queen;
darkness and impenetrable snow!
And as for standing against him:
ay, ay, ay!

Oh dear. Oh wow.
Go and lie in the snow.

Make your mind up,
silly little Kay.

Run along now,
stupid little Gerda.

There, ahead of you:
the kingdom of death.

There, behind you:
the roses are blooming.

Well, maybe they're not...
Maybe they've withered...
So what?

You'll find out soon enough.
If you can get that far.

An Old Song About The Most Important Thing

She gave us loads to drink, our motherland,
and enough to eat, more or less.
And yes, she beat us, but on the other hand,
she didn't strike with all her force.

But we did not love her, and
she did not love us.

Historiosophical

You can't know Russia with your mind.
You can't know Poland, or Albania,
Nigeria, Cuba, or Tasmania,
The Windward Islands or Britannia,
Equatorial Guinea, Hungary-Austria,
Rome or Middle-Earth or Narnia –
they're their own sort and their own kind.

All you can do is believe in Russia.
No, all you can do is believe in the Lord.
Everything else is a hopeless fraud.
However you decide to measure,
we have been granted our reward:

you can more or less live in Russia,
if you serve the Fatherland and the Tsar.

Nota Bene

I went to America. I shimmied up the skyscrapers.
I chatted with Brodsky, and he told me not ter
sign my books on the slant, because that was
vulgar and pretentious. This important advice
had been given him by Anna Andreyevna Akhmatova,
and now in turn, kids, I pass it on to ya.
A shame that, if things keep on the way they're going,
there'll be no one around for you to tell anything.

VASILY KAMENSKY

Translated by Eugene Ostashevsky, type by Daniel Mellis

These four poems come from *Tango with Cows,* a chapbook released by the Russian Futurist poet Vasily Kamensky in March 1914 in Moscow. Printed on the reverse of yellow wallpaper with flowers in white, green, red, blue, and black, *Tango with Cows* is, above all, a ground-breaking work of typographic visual poetry set in a dazzling variety of typefaces. Unlike in Russian Futurist chapbooks by other authors, printed either by lithography or letterpress, Kamensky builds most poems directly on the page, making their word games inseparable from the layout. This fact also put his book ahead of Western competition, even of Marinetti's *Zang Tumb Tumb,* published in the same month, whose textual flow is overwhelmingly linear. The American graphic artist Daniel Mellis and I have been collaborating on a typographic and poetic translation of *Tango with Cows* that will also preserve its materiality as closely as possible.

One of the founding members of what would become Russian Futurism, Kamensky took up aviation in 1911, becoming the first European poet to pilot a plane, in his case a Blériot XI. Marinetti, who had earlier flown over Milan as a passenger, had rhetorically linked air travel with the new poetic language he called *parole-in-libertà,* which strove to replace free verse. Marinetti's words-in-freedom dispensed with natural syntax to concatenate nouns, verbs in the infinitive, and standalone adjectives. The act of reading was to be aided by 'expressive typography'. It is not surprising that the Russian Futurist poet-aviator based his most avant-garde poems on Marinetti's poetics of technological modernity. Nonetheless, Kamensky's use of typography to play with the shapes and sounds of words, as opposed to reference, has no Italian parallels. Rather, it is related to the trans-sense practices of his Russian colleagues. The term Kamensky used for his production is 'ferroconcrete poems'.

There are two main types of poems in *Tango with Cows:* linear texts and nonlinear word-arrangements. The nonlinear pieces take up one side of a page, have no obvious beginning and end, are divided into sections that look like cubist planes, and are set in a frame. They are cubist pictures made with words.

The three nonlinear paintings presented here seem to record Kamensky's visits to different popular places in Moscow. They date from January or perhaps early February of 1914. In one, the poet reacts to Sergei Schukin's pioneering collection of French paintings, where, every Sunday, visitors could encounter the work of Matisse and Picasso. The Nikitin Circus, located on Tverskaya and Bolshaya Sadovaya, ran a programme in the first two weeks of January that exactly matches that of the poem, which imitates a show poster: hence the deliberate misspellings. Like other pieces in *Tango*, 'Baths' mixes what the poet perceives with what he feels as he encounters modern popular life. The dissolution of the borders between mind and world, text and image, and sound and meaning, together with rejection of textual linearity in favour of letting the poem be apprehended at once – all of these are facets of simultaneity, the most fashionable avant-garde concept of the years immediately preceding the First World War.

DARE

cocophony **of souls** phrrphrrphrr

MOTOR sym-PHO-NY

| | | futurist SONGSLINGER AND

AVIATOR-PILOT
VASILY KAMENSKY

with my elastic PROpellER

SCREWED IN THE CLOUDS

throwing down for

death SAGGY COCOTTE

a sewn from PITY

tango manteau

AND *stockings*

with bloomers

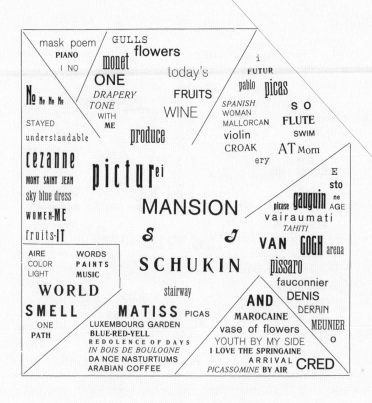

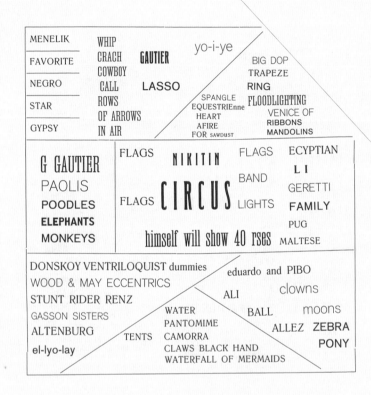

MENELIK
FAVORITE
NEGRO
STAR
GYPSY

WHIP
CRACH **GAUTIER**
COWBOY
CALL LASSO
ROWS
OF ARROWS
IN AIR

yo-i-ye

SPANGLE
EQUESTRIEnne
HEART
AFIRE
FOR sawdust

BIG DOP
TRAPEZE
RING
FLOODLIGHTING
VENICE OF
RIBBONS
MANDOLINS

G GAUTIER
PAOLIS
POODLES
ELEPHANTS
MONKEYS

FLAGS

FLAGS

NIKITIN

CIRCUS

himself will show 40 rses

FLAGS
BAND
LIGHTS

ECYPTIAN
L I
GERETTI
FAMILY
PUG
MALTESE

DONSKOY VENTRILOQUIST dummies
WOOD & MAY ECCENTRICS
STUNT RIDER RENZ
GASSON SISTERS
ALTENBURG
el-lyo-lay

TENTS

WATER
PANTOMIME
CAMORRA
CLAWS BLACK HAND
WATERFALL OF MERMAIDS

eduardo and PIBO
ALI clowns
BALL moons
ALLEZ ZEBRA
PONY

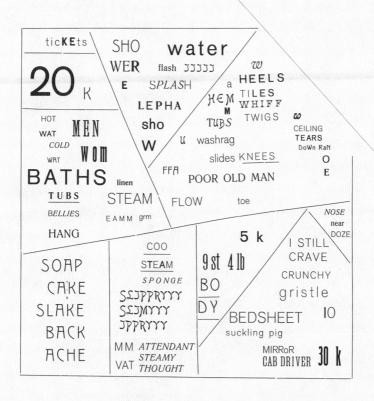

ALLA GORBUNOVA

Translated by Elina Alter

The landscapes of Alla Gorbunova's poems are both intensely
familiar and impossible to map. The cities and the semi-mythical sea
of the poems here are ephemeral and, at the same time, as acutely
specific as dreams. Like dreams, the poems invite and repel – even
repeal – interpretation.

But a map does come into being here. Chernobyl and Hiroshima,
cities that have become shorthand for the tragedies of the twentieth
century, are rebuilt a few lines away from ancient Heliopolis, and
close to towns of the literal interior: 'red cities in the mouth, on the
tongue'. A child grows up knowing only war, and falls in love with his
enemy, the 'tsar of the wooden island'. Other cities, those enormous
manifestations of labour, may come into being only for an instant,
but in that instant they have unique and specific histories, 'existing
only in the language'. Geography, chronology, and even myth are
used to compose a personal guide.

The images here are drawn from Gorbunova's lucid dreams, and
put to work in the tangible, historical project of expanding the
boundaries of poetic form in Russian. These poems were written in
2009; Gorbunova's most recent book, a collection of short prose
pieces, continues this project. Gorbunova was born in Leningrad in
1985, and now lives in Moscow. In the course of her life, the names on
Russian maps, and their corresponding meanings, have undergone a
cataclysmic change. Today the history and the loyalties of a given
place are questions with very real consequences. Elsewhere in
Gorbunova's poems, villages are abandoned, cities are chaotic, but
both hold out the possibility of transformation; it's in the personal
landscape of real that any meaningful change can take place, in
'Russia's dream of Russia'.

cities: an inventory

toy cities, made from cardboard, with colourful towers and little
figurines whose faces are indistinguishable, prop-cities for the theatre
stage, invariably bright, cities drawn from beginning to end and
placed in one italian park, cities existing only in the language,
because only in the flicker of words and the drift of sentences are
their ephemeral bodies made, and, were they displayed any other
way, it would be something different, cities desired and despised,
imaginary, created by one man on the bogs of ingria, paradise,
heliopolis and metropolis, cartoon cities – funny soviet, dreamlike
japanese, dollhouse medieval cities, where lived the brave little tailor
who killed seven at one blow, cities where nobody lives, destroyed by
the atom bomb, hiroshima and nagasaki, cities emptied by an
explosion at the nuclear power plant, chernobyl, cities which always
pain me, – and this is all cities, cities where my ancestors lived:
petropavlovsk, tula, vyatka, perm, only outside vyatka and perm
there were villages, krasnoyarsk, where denis grew up, unknown
cities, located inside beings with monstrous factories in their bellies,
red cities in the mouth, on the tongue, smirched with smog, splitting
them from the red sky-palate, cities within cities, cities i don't care
anything about, – and this is all cities, new jerusalem, finally, and
city-for-itself, unnamed and unimaginable by any living creature
– there aren't any cities.

twins

a father and his sons lived on a boat in the middle of the water. the warriors of the tsar of the wooden island in the middle of the water approached them. one of the old man's sons went to fight with them: day and night he fought by the wooden island with the tsar of the wooden island, and forgot his father and brothers, year after year he battled in water to the knee, to the waist, to the chest, as the warriors of the tsar of the wooden island pushed him farther into the water. his wooden sword rotted, but the sword of the tsar of the wooden island rotted also, the warriors of the tsar grew tired and perished, but the tsar of the wooden island and the son of the old man fought hand to hand with one another in the shallows in wet garments, and neither one had any strength remaining, they dropped one another into the water, grew drunk with the blood of one another, were smeared with sand, and the entire horizon was water, and barely noticeable in the distance was the boat of the old man, they fought year after year, hungering, swallowing small live fishes. and the tsar of the wooden island chopped off the pinky of the old man's son and ate it, and the son of the old man squeezed out the eye of the tsar of the wooden island and drank it. when the son of the old man went to fight, he was still a child, – and so he grew, seeing nothing but the tsar of the wooden island, water, albatrosses and cormorants. but then the tsar of the wooden island bashed his head with an old oar, and the son of the old man fell unconscious, and when he awoke he saw his brothers, come for him in a rowboat. they took him to his father on the boat, but the old man's son left them, and they could not hold him. his father and brothers destroyed the rowboat, so he couldn't sail away, but he walked along the water bottom and returned to the tsar of the wooden island, because he loved him, and the tsar of the wooden island loved him also, and they lay, hand in hand and lip to lip, and the water rocked the wooden island, like the pouch at the belly of a kangaroo, like the mother's womb given over to the brawling twins, where they lived and died in a day. and they still barely resembled children, just some clots. then the water tossed them ashore.

MARIA STEPANOVA

Translated by Sasha Dugdale

Russian poet Maria Stepanova wrote her epic poem 'War of the Beasts and the Animals' in 2015, when the war in the Donbas Region of Ukraine was at its height. Every line in this densely-populated and highly allusive poem emerges from a consciousness of conflict and the martial culture and mythology that allows state-sponsored violence to happen. Stepanova traces the mythmaking culture of war from ballads and films of the Russian Civil War through the Second World War and into the twenty-first century, and Russia's illegal and covert involvement in a war against Ukraine.

'War of the Beasts and the Animals' is impossible to translate in a superficially 'faithful' way: the language is so much a captive of the surrounding culture: folk refrains jostle for space against psalms, Silver Age Russian poetry, an Old Russian epic poem 'The Tale of Igor's campaign', pop ballads, phrases from popular culture, Paul Celan, T. S. Eliot – the list is endless. Many of these allusions are simply not accessible to a non-Russian audience and the challenge in translating this extraordinary poem was to find strategies to deal with this super-charged and highly specific 'modernism'.

Maria and I worked on this translation together during her residency at The Queen's College in Oxford earlier this year and I used her extensive notes and comments to guide me through. Often, where I felt an image wouldn't work in translation I could return to Maria's notes on her intended effect and choose a slightly different image, or extend the image in some way. Maria also gave me the freedom to use images with a currency in the UK, and as both Russia and Britain suffer from martial and imperial mythmaking this gave me great satisfaction. Lines from Kipling found their way into the poem, for example, and a pre-battle quote from Anthony and Cleopatra replaced a line from a Russian poem about lovers on the eve of a battle.

In the end this text is a triangulation rather than a translation. It is the result of a dance between the original poem, Maria and me, and it has at its heart Russian poet Grigory Dashevsky's concept of the existence of 'a poem's pre-textual body' from which we can both draw.

War of the Beasts and the Animals

Look, the spirits have gathered at your bedside
Speaking in Lethean tongues
Hush-a-bye, so flesh and fine,
For what do you long?

———

I smiled
He said, Marusya,
Marusya, hold on tight. And down
We went

———

No vember
the cruellest month, the hoarsest mouth
driving from the dead clay
peasants forged to the field,
cows, curs, leaving *over their dead body*
the postbag snagged in the stream

the tin spoon
the quick streams slipping the quicksilver
    slip sliding away to the estuary

◆

This little piggy went to market
And this little piggy froze to death
And the landowner put a gun to his head
And a black car came for the officer

The Greek in Odessa, the Jew in Warsaw
The callow young cavalryman
The Soviet schoolboy
Gastello the pilot
And all those who died in this land
out of the murky pool, the surface still warmed by the sun
in a night in may, steps rus al ka and quickly begins her work
throws her wet clothes from her tramples with her wet feet
her black body shines her white smock cast

mother, mother is that you? alyosha I don't rightly know

o swallow, swallow, is it her? she flew away, my friend

———

such high-minded intercourse
topples and must fall at last

a plague a both your
(ivy-clad turret, waterside folly)

masha learns on breakfast tv:
'er petticoat was yaller an' 'er little cap was green
Till apples grow on an orange tree
breaches of password security
if I were drowned in the deepest sea
thus sung the maid down in the valley

russian actor mikhail porechenkov
fingers his warm little rifle
like the latest novelty musical box
like he's desperate
to grow his own golden fleece
and the narrow water's already round his knees

svyatoslav in kiev did hear the ringing of that knell

and tom thumb
bid them listen
who were of the lands of Surozh and Korsun:

black night brings long strings
foot-foot-foot-foot slogging
all the millers-of-god

hi ho hi ho and off they go
to civil war

———

with a musket, fife and
general to the right of them
precarium in a buttonhole
wore his hair like a liberal

o your goldenes haar
        and a pair of blue eyes

not much to say
        feel free to surmise

thou art the armourer of the heart
sing me a ditty, something from rossini
rosina, perhaps, like on radio rossiye

———

as in a chariot race
the chosen one, glistening like quartz
in his roaring metal carapace
whips this way along the course
but the chariot is cleverer
throwing up stones
crashes the barrier

and crushes
the marrow from bones,

so, setting out rooks and queen
in their chequered chambers
culture leads fear
down the gauntlet of human nature,
stinking of laurel wreaths
steeped in a boiling pan,
to where there's a lively trade
in the living unit of man

sing to me of how, on an ancient alley on your family's estate,
the weathered bones lay bleached and scattered
under a birch tree; quietly they chattered:
there was no point to us, we didn't lend each other our hands
like babes we lay in the nursery in our swaddling bands

———

I can just imagine coming under him
says one, and I can hear everything

and the other is speaking, speaking

fruits of the kerbside reads the jar label
from whatever takes root in the stony rubbish
embers, sawdust, scorched wood

suspended in sweet amber sugar
cockerel-shaped lollies for the day of the dead.

when I'm off to market, or when I'm coming home
I always remember what she said back then

———

one leg crossed the other: who goes on top
one leg vows to the other: I'll top you

———

when we seize all the banks!
redistribute the fruits of our labour!
and the engines in all the tanks
flooded with rainwater
then we'll help the poor earth
shake the wig from her head
erect a polytunnel instead
with a multiplication of those poles: *cold* and *dead*
and the south will come knocking at our ears
pears will droop in the heat
gleaming bulbous pears
swollen globular fruit
and the pizza delivery's well-oiled
and the truth wears at our heart:

for the rapid soil

shall bring forth its own bard.

———

were it not seemly, citizens
to begin in ancient diction
to stay silent

———

oh in paris I could have lived and died
if there had been nowhere else besides

moscow your lands
china your waters
and those small trees in tanganyika
where the saplings and new roots are hidden
when it comes to it

somebody's been put here to keep guard over it all

here, at the crossroads
of two legs, vast, cack-footed
the un-russian god rose
the puddles reflected

to swell the goats and plump the hazel shell
the shadows under a birch like a cut out
my darling priapus, surely it's time to sprout?
or is the geist not doing so well?

nothing here corresponds to the spotted skin
and the pink dusk
comes from the time of a nation's devastation
no one calls for coolness,
                                    all want con flag ration

and here the iambs trip-trap: tetrameters chirrup
but trip up on naked vowels
and fall so far from europe
bleeding pelts, they howl

———

children in the yard play at being olympian gods
and then at gestapo interrogation – tbh it's much the same

I had a dream
night in its nuptial attire
the cornfield the melon's swelling belly
under the stars the machine gunner sings
to the machine gun,
swaddled
cradled at his breast

sleep my sunflower
sleep my poppy
soon the warm sun will come back from the south
and there'll be new life in the
pedestrian subway
playing on the half-dismembered harmony
and soldiers soldiers
gather the light ash in pots

    ———

how little earth was saved on the bosom of the earth
lift the corner of the blanket, replace the hot water bottle
measure perspiration, water allow reach for it

deep in-draught:

ditch after
dug-out

dogged   indrafted

    ———

say the word that don't belong

put it on and march along

forget the old and step anew

and the word will march with you

that word, it curls up and dies
at your lips as it emerges
like the spread-eagled toad it lies
in the heat on the verges

it clots sticky in the mouth
froths issues
here let me wipe out
it's in the tissue
ugh with it   e   u
and gagging   om
they don't half-mean anything
when they die they're gone

blue wings thrown wide
under the weight of the sky
the eagle floats over the forest
undulating in the air like a plaice

divested of alphabet

———

on the twenty-second of june
at four o'clock on the dot
I won't be listening to anything
I'll have my eyes shut

I'll bury the foreign broadcast
It's the news but I won't lift a hand
If anyone comes I'm out of the loop

I'm a sparrow   I'm no man's land

———

the home fires are burning low
be still my heart beat slow
don't spend the kerosene douse the fire
it won't end as I desire

strongly it bears us along in swelling and limitless billows
a hundred young warriors scrambling to form the watch

the warrior's raven-black horse returns without its rider
the dark cloud was without silver lining
the song snatched

from the river the bayonets glittered
glimpses of white sleeve
volunteer walking at volunteer
cigarette in the death-grip of teeth

human waves
drum bangs
machine gun strafes
camera pans

birds singing in the sycamore tree
major petrov fucks major deyev

in the coarse pockets of ploughed soil

———

that night
over the field of battle
the nachtigall tells the nachtigall
nightingasps in disbelief

and in neighbouring places
bird tells bird passing
from beak to beak like a dead frog
the exact science:
earth's caesura
between the stains of the sighted
between one mottled zone of streetlights
warmed by proximate life
and its answering beam

the sightlessness of moss on boughs
anxious flight

armoured vehicles
lenses
aimed at movement

———

no difference between first and second
patriotic or patriotic
great or pacific
atlantic
world

all the same they fall
to the only the civil
where sunrise quivers in the cinders

draws out the spear-tips

mate eh mate
giss a light
says the dead to the dead
says the killed to the killer

———

the flower dies under a skin of glass
mouth blackens stumps trickly crust

earth takes the dead she keeps them
and brings them up when she must

the sensible animals hold court
the witness box is a transparent lung
dark and trickled the way is damp
the bitch suckles her young

the judge lifts its eyes from the bench
to daylight's low-hung bulb
holds up wanted posters
and asks the jury if I am absolved

barely pausing their talk
yesterday's brothers emerge from the copse
in charred pelts, mud-crusted
get up on the cart, whip on the horse

to where the meadow holds an awning,
pins to itself a path of stings and thorns
the way back is belted down
even hope is stillborn

how to justify this? on the greedy tongue
milk writes in curds,
and paper is marked by   tree rings
traces of axe   a fool's words

magna imago

———

the acacia has long blossomed
the army is long gone
melodeclamation
                   has spread its wings and flown

ride a cock horse

to wherever the cross
and rip out the stuffing
and give it a toss
and freedom needs stripping

stay standing, lads, as long as you can
bust the joint, smash the game
one of our gang will crouch in a hole
wherever we are, and swig champagne

gypsies – dead
hussars – defunct
dusk now falls
colour shrunk

pitter patter
across the heart
sputter spatter
on the tablecloth

voices raised in lament
which once were full of joy

———

who is that riding on to red square
towards st basil's cathedral
countries rejoice cities jubilant

across my territory
begins two minutes history
vixens bark at the crimson shields

mosquitoes' drone
drowns out the pealing of bells

Russian hares
in all the polling stations
the country has spoken

and then the midges
tearing themselves from flesh
rotate tactically overhead

who wouldn't want to be drinking the quiet don from grandfather's
wooden cup, going back in time, rub your eyes
put kebabs on the fire

reclaim those words   sprinkle them on
soup

sprinkle earth

———

Vlas the volunteer, a fortnight dead
forgot the ruble rate, and what the sparrows said
and where he was from.
                     A current of explosive air
held his bones in embrace. As he flew
the years passed from him, chubby-cheeked
babbling.

             Russky or Ukrainian,
o you, whoever you are, in this neglected crossing place,
consider Vlas. Vlas was nicer than you.

———

we	no	ger	man
we	no	ger	man
on	our	off	
spring	down	grew	

no	man	we	
not	be	come	
we	no	ger	
man	rage	blood	

no   fish   we
fish   now   dumb
fish   we   can
do   deal   with

no   thing   we
no   skull   we
no   house   bird
no   cherry   tree

we   no   we   you
we   no   we   we
in   the   myrtle   grove
I   sleep   and   see

be   yond   be   hind
spoke   n   word
rush   an   bear
mel   o   dies

we   no   a
not   straight away

———

the human body
is not soap wearing thin to a hole
in the scented water bowl
nor is it ever wholly
of the past, always of the here and now

glows through the deadwood
not easy to dispatch
it creeps up like a snowdrop
through the carbon patch

and what was pining, barely alive
shut away within its bony cage
now floods into the dark recesses
to happen again

new life emerges when hope is no more
and you stand there, empty-handed and unsure

———

they travelled a long time

longlongtime

dumbstruck stillstanding trees

not-earth and earth pressed close

builder's yards   morgues   fly-tips

skyfail palewhite

bluehills skywarmed

up and down the road and the road

swallet
grim
droop
spinybroom
steep
stonecrop
cumb

the unbending river Vodopr'
can't swallow enough water –
its shame next to the
perfectly round hills

they call the hills 'mounts'
and we walked on the mount
we strolled in ornamental gardens
reflected in the long shanks of birch
we gazed in the heavenly blue
we noticed that populousness is bluer:
roofs fences

cars
heavy colours like a waterproof tarp

no one from our family
has been in these lands
since nineteen sixteen

glare of white handkerchiefs
spread wide
on the uncharted waters

non op posing
non meta morph osing
non harvest table
non stop able

———

life, you are a gash in need of stitching
death, you are a crust that yearns for filling

———

those who carry in their mouths, at first with care, heads with seeing eyes

those who touched newspaper print in their heads, as mother said never
     to do, never, wash your hands

those who rip apart in flight, carrying from nest to nest, smearing on
     the glass

attempt to mount the blunt-snouted body on a set of wheels,

set it trundling, throat outstretched and spouting fire

yes, them and these, too
but actually more these

for them conscripts spread their green arms wide
like a tablecloth plentifully spread
lie heaped at their feet like birch logs
to please the valkyries
at the harpies' hearts desire
to the bayan's thrum
the accordion's reveille

and O, those children's voices, singing where once there was a dome
in the soiled field
surrounded by corn and scarecrows

———

not on the earth but above or below
war's deep grunt
producing slimy rivers of sweat
its hand feels for the gut

and we   stagger
carry ourselves through the darkness

and mother demeter mithering in the muck
and anguish of the fields
hears from below: mother fuck
yet the sky might be brightening, or so it feels

and mother hecate comes out for a smoke
from the back street
from the foul black streets from the pecking fowl
the puddles of spilt milk

the earth lying like a kitbag
behind enemy lines   give it tongue
mother mary hurries
but hasn't yet come

————

in the wind's spirit
the still small voice of cold
she, who cradles leviathan in her hands, like the infant
and she who rises above the rye
all are present for this, as it happens
they watch, they steadily

unspeaking

as the ice in the ice house and the tear in the bottle come of age
as the soil tastes the first weight of the rain
as the ice-stoves send out blocks of
smoking death
in the big brother house a fight opens like a flower

women in flip-flops
fixated
shut the fuck up why don't

spring in the recruiting office
knee jerk, stethoscope down the spine
picking out the shaggy the short-legged the sinewy
under matron's watchful eye

how the thick plaits of herring stream away
the lines of tanks on bridges flash in the sun
a waiter's flourish reveals a pitiful morsel
shivering, drizzled in salt, underdone

and over there is everything that I kiss from afar
that I love to smithereens
all of it still shouting alleluia
but no respite from the shameful dream

serpents and all deeps
tin soldiers at the city walls
all the ranks of angels
nanny lena digging vegetables
snow like wool and hoarfrost like ashes
throat like spindrift, legs like a foal
heart thrust through the noose
like a button through a button hole

save us from the right hand of falsehood

a memory
won't save us
lies in the ashes
biting its own tail

he taketh not pleasure in the legs of a man
nor the strength of a horse

———

like the tailor who sews
not the straitjacket
(which from childhood has begged to sit up
woken from the canvas)
but the pattern
cuts on the bias

and the dress isn't tight
just itchy

like a court proceeding
down the long hospital corridor
with a heavy trolley
handing out the tightly wrapped packages
the little living weights of verdicts

three per cord, ladies

like when in a moment's confusion you spit out a barbed word

and it lodges in a treebody
or the body of a comrade
or a friendlip
and the line
goes taut

fish hooks a fish

like a mound
under a snowdrift
means nothing
writing on a tomb
sees no one
writing on a stone
nothing, we read
it not

but it is

REVIEWS

Songs From A Flooded Valley

Stray Truths: Selected Poems of Euphrase Kezilahabi, edited and translated by Annmarie Drury, Michigan Sate University Press, 2015

In his 1988 poem 'The Seed' Euphrase Kezilahabi addresses his near-contemporary, traditionalist Swahili poet Amiri A Sudi Andanenga in clear terms: 'The time has passed when grey hairs were wisdom | and rhymes a poem; | now is a time when ideas rule.' Born in a fishing village far from the coastal heartland of traditional Swahili verse, Kezilahabi had by this time already gained a significant reputation as a free-verse innovator with the publication of his 1974 collection *Kichomi* (A Painful Twinge). As Annmarie Drury's very useful contextualising introduction to *Stray Truths* tells us, that debut collection drew strong censure from Swahili formalists who saw the defections of Western influence in the perceived impurity of its modernising aesthetic. In the newly-united and independent Tanzania, Kezlahabi was writing in Swahili in ways that aimed to bring *lugha ya kila siku* – the language of every day – into what had until then principally been a highly stylised poetic conversation:

> Andanenga, brother Andanenga,
> new seeds have sprouted
> and others are ripening on the tree...

> Those old forms hang loosely on the syllable-poets...
> You'll be buried in great museums!
> And above your graves we'll write
> 'Traditional poets.'

Euphrase Kezilahabi has been a key figure in Tanzanian writing now for over four decades. Annmarie Drury's selection of around fifty of Kezilahabi's poems, presented in translation alongside their originals, at last offers English-language readers an opportunity to fully appreciate the central place his work holds in contemporary East African literature, at a time when Swahili has become a modern *lingua franca* across the wider region. Several of the better-known poems translated here have appeared over the years in individual translations into a number of languages – including as part of a Poetry Translation Centre project in London, working with the Finnish writer and Swahili scholar Katriina Ranne. But *Stray Truths* is the first really comprehensive selection in English and constitutes a valuable curation of his poetry to date, in support of which Drury was awarded a PEN Translation Fund grant in 2011.

In poems from three collections 1974–2008, Kezilahabi writes with clear-eyed and often wry lyricism about everyday life for the individual in the fast-changing world of post-independence Tanzania. These are poems about hope and about hopelessness, embedded in imagery as material in its evocations as it is symbolic: water and rain, trees and crops, roads and power lines. Poems from his first two collections sharply describe the challenges of development in the new nation, after the radical drive towards *Ujamaa*, Julius Nyerere's socialist vision announced in the landmark Arusha Declaration, or Resolution, of 1967. Drury's translation of 'Azimio' ('Resolution'), worth quoting in its short entirety, delivers all the dismay and disappointment of Kezilahabi's original:

The Resolution now is leftover food
on the capitalist's mustache,
a pen that leaks

in the student's bag,
heavy dust
after cows have passed.
No one was shaven,
no one was given a new pen
and the road was not sealed.
What remains now
are some millet grains
scattered in the desert
by a blind sower.

Other poems are still more bitter in tone: 'News came from Arusha |
and we started sorting the rice of *ujamaa...* || When will we eat without
the stones, without the broken grains?' ('Sorting the Rice'). And later
from the same 1974 collection, 'Knife in Hand' meditates on the taboo
subject of despair and suicide:

Knife, an unholy life, this,
if to look backward or ahead
is completely to lose heart!

A highly-regarded novelist as well as a poet, Kezilhabi's political
and philosophical ideas come to life poetically in scenes which are as
dramatic as they are pointed. In the memorable 'Floods' ('Mafuriko'),
the poet sings about a flooded valley where the electricity poles are
all down, and in the darkness the old houses stand threatened by
over-leaning trees. It's a scene – like many others in *Stray Truths* –
which the poet sees as already a moment in history that will be sung
of in future songs: 'We'll be left telling our grandchildren: "That
year of the flood | many of our first trees fell" || This year's flood! |

Many people will be undone.'" From the same powerful 1988 collection
Welcome Inside (Karibu Ndani), the fine poem 'A Cry in the Village'
(Kilio Kijijini) is almost filmic in its elegiac, metaphorical scene of
communal mourning against the setting of wind and storm, beautifully
translated by Drury:

> Dew has soaked the trouser hems
> of an old man arriving now amid the wailing.
> Nothing here believes in itself
> except the rainwater
> flowing swiftly towards the valley'

In the evidence of the setting, we observe the effects of powerful
forces over which individual and community seem to have little
control:

> Outside on the farm, cornstalks lie heaped on one another
> showing from where it came, the wind of death...
> Silence in the village, silence outside the houses;
> inside, cries of the bent cornstalks.

'A Cry in the Village' is a good example of Drury's attentive and
often subtly musical translation, the approach to which she describes
interestingly in her introduction: 'As translator, I had to grapple
with my anxieties about the estrangement of this narrative poetry
from a lyric tradition dominant in English.' She writes also about
her conversations with Kezilhabi over the selection of material and
his strong feeling that the several longer elegiac pieces, with their
connection to the oral traditions of his childhood, should be included.
In the event these poems contribute significantly to our understanding

not just of the poet's own 'lost' Tanzania but provide us importantly with a vivid and concrete sense of the realities on the ground more widely during the decades of nation-building. We appreciate Kezilahabi's presence too in the dual-language presentation. For the non-Swahili-speaking reader, a glance at the facing-page originals gives us a feel for the forward-spinning energy of the highly alliterative and assonant patterning, the reduplications and fluid penultimate-syllable stresses of the poet's rhythms : 'Kisha nitacheza ngoma yangu kimyakimya | Katika uwanja huu mpana uliochawa wazi...' – 'Then I'll dance my silent dance | in this broad, open field...' ('Silent Dance')

Kezilahabi's is a free verse poetics that plays arrestingly with a range of wry enquiry and exclamation, meditation and rhetorical attack, across a range of volume and mood. That's an expressive dynamic which Drury captures well in her translations of many of the key poems, not least in the 'The Moth', from 1988:

It's dark out, and an owl
hoots like a brave soldier, singing
a song of fear and death:
They brought us light to eat in the darkness.
And like an owl of the forest I reply:
To eat us in the darkness they brought us a forest

In that early poem 'Knife in Hand' the poet contemplates the violence of despair but ends by choosing 'the throb of my heart | – this throb – the very music of life.' It's an idea to which Kezilahabi's imagination remains dedicated ('I'll write a song on the wings of a fly.... On the walls of bathrooms, offices, classrooms') no matter how resigned some of the later poems appear as they speak more frequently of silence and of putting down the pen: 'I've already petitioned for my little space. | Poets, I come without a pen...' ('Namagondo III'). As Annemarie Drury admits, the final poem in this fascinating and stirring selection is both the most experimental in form and the simplest to translate:

Pa!   Pa!   Pa!
     (Silence)
Pa!

Jane Draycott

The Past as a Wounded Soldier

When They Broke Down the Door by Fatemeh Shams, translated by Dick Davis, Mage Publishers, 2016

This moving dual-language poetry collection by the Iranian exiled poet Fatemeh Shams is her first collection in English and is translated from the Persian by the eminent Persian scholar Dick Davis. Shams has previously published two collections in Persian: *88* (2013) and *Writing in the Mist* (2015). Sham's first collection of poetry in English represents an emotional journey that many follow in exile. A recurring theme is the visceral anguish of exile from Iran and the shifting forms of memory pervaded by motifs of blood, death, executions and corpses.

The first two poems in the collection are indicative of the regime under which Shams lived. Her hometown is Mashad and the imagery she uses expresses her innate repulsion for the regime's acts and values: 'I come from a town of beheaded closed cafés [...] polluted by two strands of a woman's hair | Two strands! [...] from the place of my own martyrdom'. 'When They Broke Down the Door', the shocking title poem, describes the morality police bursting into the private space where the poet and her lover are passionately entwined. The male is then beaten unconscious but the poetic persona suffers vicariously imagining her body dripping blood. The final couplet stuns the reader both because of the revelation that the male was hanged, and because of the manner in which it is revealed: parenthetically, almost as an afterthought.

Following the Green Movement uprising in 2009, Shams, who was studying in England, was unable to return to Iran because of her own writings in support of the movement and because of her backing for human rights activists. She found herself effectively in exile. She represents exile as a state of despair and of utter destabilisation. Rootless, deprived of a homeland and lacking shared memory or meaning with those who remain in Iran, she perpetually longs for the things she will never see 'If then, in all my life, I'll never see my home again | I'll creep into a cloud and pour forever there as rain'. Her sensibility is of confinement and imprisonment as she is restricted to exile and cannot return to Iran and even struggles to retain her memory of the past. This sentiment of a fading past distorted by memory is beautifully conveyed in the metaphor of a wounded soldier: 'My past | is like a wounded soldier | from a long war | who returns with one arm'... 'I don't know him anymore'. Indeed, the scholar André Aciman uses the metaphor of the exiled person's imagined amputated body part which remained behind, such as an arm, to express the visceral feeling of being bereft and longing to be whole again. In the poetic persona's deeply troubled state she likens herself to a soulless body and a corpse: 'a shroud conceals your face' and 'I sleep in my own corpse's arms'. The poems suggest that mourning and the sense of loss continue unabated.

In 'Three Years Later' the cause of her inability to fall asleep is revealed. Her trauma is associated with the Green Revolution and is caused by the violence and oppression inflicted on those involved, including her own sister who was imprisoned. She remembers the aftermath of the Green uprising: 'From someone missing at the roadside, three years before | To the destroyed, hidden graves of the slain, three years later [...] the burning ashes still remain, three years later' and 'suffering the wounds that we bore inside'.

Many of the poems here articulate her desperate desire and passion for her lost lover in Iran: Shams experiences a double loss as exile and the loss of her lover are intertwined. Her work can be considered subversive in an Iranian context as she dares to express feminine desire, articulating her intimate feelings of love and sexuality and constructing men as her poetic subjects and as objects of love, passion and sexual desire. The influence of the work of the Iranian woman poet, Forugh Farrokhzad (1935–1967) is palpable. Iranian intellectual society strongly disapproved of Farrokhzad's poetry, accusing her of immorality as they deemed her representation of the female totally taboo and derided her for her sexual encounters and non-conformist life.

Shams expresses her love and desire for her absent lover by drawing on the imagery of Persian mystic poetry and particularly work by Rumi and Hafez. These mystics are tormented because of their separation from the loved one who is God, the ultimate Beloved. As their sublime love remains unrequited, they finally attain a euphoric state of submergence of the self. Shams uses the traditional allegorical imagery to express her love as intoxication: 'your body's wine each night', 'the wine glass slips from our lips', 'resolve my night in wine', 'I became your beloved' and 'moments of drunkenness' but she also subverts it by creating negative images of the mystic symbols of euphoria which include: 'my garden now a withered yellow site', 'the mirror bury the night', 'the sorrow of a wingless bird', 'my lonely wings were flapping wildly'.

Dick Davis's translations are sensitive and beautifully poetic and the collection includes poems in both traditional Persian and free verse forms. For the poems in traditional form he has imitated aspects of that form in English. It is intriguing to learn that poet and translator never met as Davis was living in the mid-west of America while Shams lived in London and so they conducted all their poetry translation conversations by e-mail. Dick Davis could not be present at the 2016 book launch but sent some words: 'Trying to translate her poems has been a sobering but heartening experience for me; sobering because of the obvious pain that the poems embody, but heartening because her words call on those who live unmarked by horror to listen, and in this way they can give others who share her situation some courage and hope that the world at large will not remain indifferent.'

Jennifer Langer

Poetry Roaming the Street of Language

The Missing Rib: Collected Poems 1973–2015 by K. Satchidanandan, Poetrywala, 2016

K. Satchidanandan (28 May 1946–) writes poems in his mother tongue, Malayalam, and often translates the originals into English, his poetry moving seamlessly from one language to another without losing any of its immediacy. His *Collected Poems, 1965–2005*, in three volumes, consisting of 1,400 pages, appeared in 2006. *While I Write, New and Selected Poems*, in English was published in 2011. *The Missing Rib* is a substantial and welcome addition to the poet's oeuvre in English.

Satchidanandan's poetry reflects Life in all its splendour and horror. The poems are fascinating studies of human nature in its many avatars, whilst his poetry overall is a powerful mix of the real, surreal, male, female, existential, political, intellectual, spiritual, sensual, historical, cultural, individual and universal. As someone who grew up talking to cats and crows and trees and communicated with gods and spirits, his work is characterized by a deep connectedness with nature in all its forms, 'the cornstalk and the peepal leaf' identified as his 'humble insignia'. In 'That's all', a poem from 2011, he sums up his work:

> Like a dog marking
> its passage with piss
> I mark my passage
> with words that smell life:
> that's all.

Straddling many worlds – poet, translator, teacher, editor, critic, researcher – his work is enriched by his immersion in world literature.

His readings range from the great Malayalam writers in original to translations of major Indian writers, the treasures of European and English literature, not forgetting modern poetry from all over the world. He writes of how reading the Holy Bible had a 'lasting impact' on his 'vision and imagination'. The list of influences is inclusive and comprehensive – from the *Mahabharata* to *The Communist Manifesto*. These books shaped his moral sensibility and ethical imagination. Translating works of world literature into Malayalam (his collections of world poetry in translation amount to 1,700 pages), he was also unconsciously internalising an emerging modern sensibility which is reflected in his own creations, his poetic journey helping him to explore issues relating to what it means to be human, find one's place in the world.

Commenting on the nature of poetry, he writes: 'My readings across the globe have helped reaffirm my faith in the power of poetry to speak to people across nations, languages and communities; it is the shared mother-tongue of human beings that survived the Babel. No wonder it has survived Plato's Republic, Hitler's Auschwitz and Stalin's Gulag, and still whispers its uneasy truths into the human ear trained through centuries to capture the most nuanced of voices.' The same is true of his poetry, its ability to rise above passing fashions by appealing to the truth of being human, asking questions that have concerned mankind through the ages – the meaning of life, freedom, choice, immortality, time, love, death, nature, language.

In this poem 'Stammer' we have one such unforgettable encounter:

Stammer is no handicap.
It is a mode of speech.

Stammer is the silence that falls
between the word and its meaning,

just as lameness is the
silence that falls between the word and the deed.

His poems, pared down to essentials, convey a message that is universal, a vision of poetry that is timeless.

He acknowledges the limitation of words: 'Nothingness is a pure language', he writes in 'Words', reinforcing the idea in 'Languages'. In 'The State of Poetry' he describes the degraded state of poetry, 'now dumb, roams | the street of language, begging' where 'the market rapes her'. He speaks of the struggle for freedom, rages against the injustices of the world, the pressing need for it 'to be remade by imagination'.

The collection includes an essay by the author about his life and poetry; a chronology of his life is also provided. The poems are grouped into eleven sections, and each poem is assigned a year. It is not self-evident if the year refers to their composition in Malayalam, translation into English or publication. A brief note on the compilation, sources of the author's books where they first appeared, would have provided insight into the poet's creative process and evolution as a writer, though the lack of it is no impediment to the reader's journey in losing and finding himself in these poems.

Shanta Acharya

NOTES ON CONTRIBUTORS

SHANTA ACHARYA is the author of eleven books. Her latest, *Imagine: New and Selected Poems*, is published by HarperCollins (India), 2017. www.shantaacharya.com

ARON AJI'S translations include three book-length works by Karasu: *Death in Troy*; *The Garden of Departed Cats*, (2004 National Translation Award); and *A Long Day's Evening*, (NEA Literature Fellowship, and short-listed for the 2013 PEN Translation Prize). He is the current president of The American Literary Translators Association.

ELINA ALTER is a writer and translator in New York. Her work appears in *The Paris Review Daily*, *Guernica*, *Slice*, *BOMB*, *The Southeast Review*, and *Brooklyn Magazine*.

CONSUELO ARIAS has published critical essays on the construction of the queer subject in Spanish and Spanish-American literature: 'Writing the Female Body in the Texts of Cristina Peri Rossi: Excess, Monumentality and Fluidity' (2000) and '(Un)veiling Desire: Configurations of Eros in the Poetry of Jaime Gil de Biedma' (1993).

POLINA BARSKOVA is a Saint Petersburg-born poet, prose writer, and scholar. She has authored ten collections of poems in Russian; three collections in English translation, *This Lamentable City* (2010), *The Zoo in Winter* (2010), and *Relocations* (2013); and a collection of short stories in Russian, *The Living Pictures* (2014), for which she was awarded the Andrey Bely Prize (2015).

BEVERLEY BIE BRAHIC'S collection, *White Sheets,* was shortlisted for the 2012 Forward Prize; *Hunting the Boar* (2016) was a Poetry Book Society Recommendation, and her translation, *Guillaume Apollinaire, The Little Auto,* won the 2013 Scott Moncrieff Prize. beverleybiebrahic.com

UILLEAM BLACKER is a lecturer in comparative culture of Eastern Europe at the School of Slavonic and East European Studies, University College London. His translations of the work of contemporary Ukrainian writers have appeared on *Words Without Borders*, in the *Dalkey Archive Best European Fiction* series, and in the journal *Ukrainian Literature in Translation*. He is also a member of the UK-based Ukrainian theatre group *Molodyi Teatr London*.

LEONARDO BOIX is an Argentinean journalist and poet based in London and Deal (Kent). He has published two collections in Spanish. His English poems have appeared in *The Rialto, Minor Literature[s], The Morning Star, Ink, Sweat and Tears*, and elsewhere. He is currently a member of The Complete Works III.

BERTOLT BRECHT, one of the twentieth century's finest dramatists and lyric poets, was born in Germany and forced into exile in 1933, when the National Socialists took power. A full English-language *Collected Poems* is due out with Norton-Liveright in 2018, in translations by David Constantine and Tom Kuhn.

DIONISIO CAÑAS, a native of Spain, has published many books of poetry, essays on contemporary Hispanic/Latino art and literature as well as short stories. Cañas has also been active in performance, video, video-poetry, digital poetry, installation and art criticism.

CHIKAKO NIHEI has recently completed a doctoral thesis on the novels of Murakami Haruki at the University of Sydney. She is currently a lecturer at Yamaguchi University in Japan and is working on a publication concerning Murakami and literary translation.

DAVID CONSTANTINE will publish a new and greatly enlarged selection of his translations of Hölderlin's poetry with Bloodaxe next year.

ALINA DADAEVA was born in 1989 in Dhizak (Uzbekistan). Her work has appeared in Russian, Uzbek, Ukrainian and US journals and anthologies. Her translations from English and Spanish into Russian have appeared in several journals, including *Interpoeziia*.

JANE DRAYCOTT'S latest collections are *The Occupant* (Carcanet 2016, PBS Recommendation) and *Storms Under the Skin,* translations of selected poems and prose poems 1927-1954 by artist and poet Henri Michaux (Two Rivers Press 2017, PBS Recommended Translation), both including work first published in *MPT.*

ARIANE DREYFUS (b.1958) has published over fifteen collections of poetry, including *La durée des plantes* (Tarabuste, 1998), *L'inhabitable* (Flammarion, 2006, awarded the *Prix des découvreurs* in 2007). The poems translated here are from her latest collection *Le dernier livre des enfants* (Flammarion, 2016).

JORGE EDUARDO EIELSON was born in Lima, Perú. He published fourteen collections of poetry, two novels and four books of essays. His work as a visual artist was exhibited at the Venice Biennale, Documenta, and MOMA. He won the National Poetry Award (1944) and the National Drama Award (1948). He wrote in Spanish and Italian.

TATIANA FILIMONOVA has published articles on contemporary Russian writers such as Vladimir Sorokin and Pavel Krusanov, as well as on contemporary film.

AMELIA M. GLASER is an associate professor of Russian and comparative literature at the University of California San Diego. Her most recent publication (as editor) is *Stories of Khmelnytsky: Competing Literary Legacies of the 1648 Ukrainian Cossack Uprising* (Stanford University Press, 2015).

ALLA GORBUNOVA was born in Leningrad in 1985. A poet, prose-writer, critic and translator, she has published five books of poetry and one book of short prose.

DAVID GRAMLING translates from German and Turkish. He has translated Zafer Şenocak, Sabahattin Ali, Murathan Mungan, Bejan Matur, Ersan Üldes, Peter Waterhouse, and Menekşe Toprak, selections of which have been published *in The American Reader, Words Without Borders, TRANSIT, the PEN Translation Slam*, and the *Nazim Hikmet Poetry Festival* book.

DAVID HARSENT has published eleven volumes of poetry. *Legion* won the Forward Prize for best collection; *Night* won the Griffin International Poetry Prize. His most recent collection, *Fire Songs*, won the T.S. Eliot Prize. A new collection, *Salt*, will be published in October 2017.

FRIEDRICH HÖLDERLIN (1770–1843) was a classical poet in his love of Ancient Greece and his mastery of antique poetic forms; and a Romantic in his loves and friendships and his longing for a humane society here and now.

ANDREW HOUWEN is a translator of Dutch and Japanese poetry and is currently a British Academy/JSPS post-doctoral fellow at Tokyo Women's Christian University. Some of his translations from the Dutch poet Esther Jansma were published in *Modern Poetry in Translation* and *Shearsman*. His own poetry has appeared in the *Oxonian Review*.

YULIYA ILCHUK has published articles on the topics of postcolonial theory and criticism, institutions of authorship, reading culture, protest art, and post-Soviet identity. Currently, she is working on a book project, titled *Nikolai Gogol: Performing Hybridity*.

ANDREW JANCO is a digital scholarship librarian at Haverford College. He holds a PhD in history from the University of Chicago. With Olga Livshin, he has translated a number of Russian and Ukrainian poets. His translations are published in *Contemporary Russian Poetry: An Anthology* and several journals.

OLENA JENNINGS'S collection of poetry *Songs from an Apartment* was released in January 2017 by Underground Books. Her translations of poetry from Ukrainian can be found in *Chelsea*, *Poetry International* and *Wolf*. She has published fiction in *Joyland*, *Pioneertown*, and *Projectile*.

FRANCIS R. JONES translates poetry, especially from Bosnian-Croatian-Serbian and Dutch into English. These translations have won several prizes – including the 2013 John Dryden Translation Competition, for early poems by Ivan V. Lalić. He lives in Northumberland, and is Professor of Translation Studies at Newcastle University.

KATERYNA KALYTKO has published six collections of poetry and one novel. She is an acclaimed translator who translates Bosnian, Croatian, and Serbian works into Ukrainian. Kalytko is also the founder of the Intermezzo Short Story Festival, the only festival in Ukraine exclusively dedicated to the short story.

VASILY KAMENSKY (1884–1961) was the first European poet-pilot. After falling out of the sky during a stunt show, he partnered with Mayakovsky and Burliuk on their winter 1913-14 tour of provincial cities. He later became a Soviet writer but survived.

ILYA KAMINSKY was born in Odessa. He is the author of *Dancing in Odessa* (Tupelo Press) which won the Whiting Writer's Award, the American Academy of Arts and Letters' Metcalf Award, the Dorset Prize, and the Ruth Lilly Fellowship. Poems from his new manuscript, *Deaf Republic*, were awarded *Poetry* Magazine's Levinson Prize and the Pushcart Prize.

HELENA KERNAN grew up in London and studied Russian and French at the University of Cambridge, where she carried out research on Armenian-Georgian filmmaker Sergei Parajanov. She has lived in Moscow, St. Petersburg and Paris.

BORIS KHERSONSKY was born in Chernivtsi in 1950. In 1999 Khersonsky became chair of the department of clinical psychology at the Odessa National University. Khersonsky has published seventeen collections of poetry and essays in Russian, and most recently, in Ukrainian. He is widely regarded as one of Ukraine's most prominent Russian-language poets.

TIMUR KIBIROV (1955–) became famous as an underground poet in the late 1980s and has only been published openly since the 1990s. He has published thirteen collections of poetry.

OSTAP KIN has published work in *The Common, Poetry International, St. Petersburg Review, Springhouse, Trafika Europe, Ohio Edit*, and in anthologies. He has edited the anthology *New York Elegies: Ukrainian Poetry on the City* (forthcoming with Academic Studies Press).

ELENA KOSTYLEVA has published two poetry collections, *Legko dostalos'* and *Lidia* (both Kolonna Publications), the second of which saw her shortlisted for the Andrey Bely prize, Russia's most prestigious independent award for literature, in 2009. Her poem 'The Language of Violence' was recently translated into English for publication in the literary journal *n+1*.

JOHANNES KÜHN is a German poet, born on February 3, 1934 in Thoely in Saarland in the south-west of Germany, where he still lives. He has published numerous collections of lyric poetry, his latest being *Und hab am Gras mein Leben gemessen* (Hanser Verlag, 2014).

TOM KUHN teaches German literature at the University of Oxford where he is a Fellow of St Hugh's College. *Brecht. Collected Poems*, edited and translated with David Constantine, is due out with Norton-Liveright in 2018.

IVAN V. LALIĆ was born in Belgrade, the Serbian and Yugoslav capital, in 1931. Though he is now celebrated as one of Serbia's best twentieth-century poets, Lalić regarded himself not just as a Serbian or a Yugoslav poet, but also – primarily, even – as a Mediterranean poet. He died in Belgrade in 1996.

JENNIFER LANGER, founding director of Exiled Writers Ink, is a poet and editor of four anthologies of exiled literature, most recently: *If Salt has Memory: Jewish Exiled Writing* (2008) all published by Five Leaves. She holds a doctorate in Iranian literature of exile and is a School of Oriental and African Studies Research Associate.

OLGA LIVSHIN is an English-language poet, essayist, and literary translator. Born in Odessa and raised in Moscow, she came to the United States as a teenager with her family. Her work has been recognized by the *CALYX* journal's Lois Cranston Memorial Prize, the Poets & Patrons Chicagoland Contest, the Cambridge Sidewalk Poetry Project, and the Robert Fitzgerald Translation Prize (twice).

OKSANA LUTSYSHYNA is a Ukrainian writer and translator. Her original work includes two novels, a collection of short stories, and three collections of poetry, all published in Ukraine. Her most recent novel has been long-listed for the Ukrainian BBC award.

VASYL MAKHNO is a poet, essayist, and translator. He is the author of eleven collections of poetry. His most recent collection, *A Paper Bridge*, appeared in 2017. He has also published two book of essays: *The Gertrude Stein Memorial Cultural and Recreation Park* (2006) and *Horn of Plenty* (2011), and two plays: *Coney Island* (2006) and *Bitch/Beach Generation* (2007).

OKSANA MAKSYMCHUK is the author of two award-winning books of poetry in the Ukrainian language, *Xenia* (2005) and *Catch* (2009). Her translations from Ukrainian and Russian have appeared in the *Best European Fiction* series (Dalkey Archive Press), *London Magazine, Words Without Borders, Poetry International*, and others. She is a co-editor of *Words for War: New Poems from Ukraine*, a NEH-funded anthology of poetry (forthcoming).

SIMON MARTIN read German and English Literature at The Queen's College, Oxford, and lives in Oxford and Berlin with his young family.

OLIVIA MCCANNON'S poetry collection *Exactly My Own Length* (Carcanet/OxfordPoets, 2011) was shortlisted for the Seamus Heaney Centre Prize and won the 2012 Fenton Aldeburgh First Collection Prize. She lived for nine years in France and her translations include Balzac's *Old Man Goriot* (Penguin Classics, 2011).

DANIEL MELLIS makes artist's books and other text-based artworks on such topics as the poetry of philosophy, the phenomenology of space, the built environment, and the law.

AINSLEY MORSE is a scholar, teacher and translator of Russian and former Yugoslav literatures.

STEPH MORRIS is a poet and translator, now based in London after years in Berlin. He was poet in residence at Bonnington Square, in 2016, and House of Saint Barnabas, in 2017, as part of Mixed Borders.

MURATHAN MUNGAN has published poetry, short stories, plays, novels, screenplays, radio plays, essays and criticism. A selection of his poems were translated and published in Kurdish as *Li Rojhilatê Dilê Min* (In the East of My Heart). His tour de force *Mesopotamian Trilogy* of plays has enjoyed successful theatre runs across the country and Europe.

NAKA TARŌ is a Japanese poet and winner of the Saisei Murō and Yomiuri poetry prizes. His experiences of the Second World War feature prominently in his début collection *Etudes* (1950). In addition to his poetry, he has written a Nō play, *Shikōtei* ('Shi Huangdi', 2003), and is also known for his critical work on the poet Hagiwara Sakutarō.

BRONKA NOWICKA is a film and theatre director, screenwriter and visual artist. She explores new media, human-object relations and language. Her first poetry collection, *To Feed The Stone* (2015), won the 2016 NIKE Prize. Her new book, *Regnum*, is forthcoming in 2018.

HELGA OLSHVANG was born in Moscow, but has lived and worked in the United States since 1996 as a writer, poet and a filmmaker. Her books include: *96th Book, The Reed, Poetry Works, Versions of the Present, The Three* and *Blue is White*.

EUGENE OSTASHEVSKY is a poet and translator specializing in word play. His latest book is *The Pirate Who Does Not Know the Value of Pi*.

THIRUNAVUKKARASU RAVINTHIRAN was born in Batticaloa in 1944, the second child of five. He was educated in postcolonial Sri Lanka in a Jesuit institution (St Michael's), before studying in India to become a doctor. He moved to England in 1976 and practised medicine for over twenty years before retiring.

VIDYAN RAVINTHIRAN is the author of *Grun-tu-molani* (Bloodaxe, 2014), shortlisted for a few prizes, and *Elizabeth Bishop's Prosaic*, winner of the University English prize and the Warren-Brooks Award for Literary Criticism. He is an editor at the online magazine of poetry and poetics, *Prac Crit*.

YANNIS RITSOS (Monemvasia 1 May 1909 – Athens 11 November 1990) was a left-wing activist and an active member of the Greek Resistance during the Second World War. He was also one of the great Greek poets of the twentieth century and his work has been widely translated into English.

MAX ROSOCHINSKY is a poet and translator from Simferopol, Crimea. His poems were nominated for the PEN International New Voices Award in 2015. With Maksymchuk, he won first place in the 2014 Brodsky-Spender competition, and co-edited a NEH-funded anthology *Words for War: New Poems from Ukraine* (Academic Studies Press, 2017).

BELA SHAYEVICH is a Soviet-American writer, artist, and translator.

IRYNA SHUVALOVA is a prize-winning Ukrainian poet and translator currently doing her PhD at the University of Cambridge, where she focuses on oral poetry in the war-affected communities.

MALLIHA SINNIAH was born in 1946 in Batticaloa, Sri Lanka. She completed her schooling in her home town, and went to university in South India, obtaining a Bachelor of Science in Mathematics and Physics. Her mother was a strong mentor and role model for her during her student years, serving as headmistress of the school Malliha attended.

OSTAP SLYVYNSKY a poet, translator, essayist, and literary critic. He was awarded the Antonych Literary Prize (1997), the Hubert Burda Prize for young poets from Eastern Europe (2009), and the Kovaliv Fund Prize (2013). In 2015, he collaborated with composer Bohdan Sehin on a media performance, *Preparation*, dedicated to the civilian victims of war in the East of Ukraine.

JOHN SMELCER'S poems have appeared in *MPT* many times over the past few decades and his work appears in *Centres of Cataclysm* (Bloodaxe, 2016). John Smelcer was a friend of the poet and founder of *MPT*, Ted Hughes.

NICOLA SAMONOV is an acclaimed Russian artist, illustrator and set and costume designer for theatre and films.

MARIA STEPANOVA is a poet, essayist, journalist and the author of ten poetry collections and two books of essays. She has been awarded several Russian and international literary awards (including the prestigious Andrey Bely Prize and Joseph Brodsky Fellowship). Her current project *In Memory of Memory* is a book-length study in the field of cultural history.

TINA STROHEKER has published several collections of poetry, two arising from her regular visits to Poland, as well as travel journals, short fiction and critical prose. She lives in Eislingen, Germany where she curated a poetry installation along a walk through the town.

CHRISTOPHE TARKOS was born in Marseille in 1963 and died in 2004. Of himself he says: 'I don't exist. I fabricate poems'; 'I am slow, extremely slow'; 'I am in and out of psychiatric institutions.' Tarkos published many books and recordings with small publishers. Éditions P.O.L. published his *Écrits Poètiques* in 2008.

ANTON TENSER was born in Novosibirsk and lived in Kiev until immigrating to the United States in 1989. As a linguist, Anton specializes in the Romani (Gypsy) language; he described the grammar of the Lithuanian Romani dialect, and authored several articles on Romani language and ethnography.

SUSAN WICKS is a poet and fiction writer. Her translations of Valérie Rouzeau, *Cold Spring in Winter* and *Talking Vrouz* (Arc), have won the Scott Moncrieff and Oxford-Weidenfeld Prizes and been shortlisted for the Popescu Prize and the International Griffin Prize for Poetry. Her own seventh collection, *The Months* (Bloodaxe, 2016) was a Poetry Book Society Recommendation.

ELŻBIETA WÓJCIK-LEESE writes with/in English, Polish
and Danish. Her poems have appeared in *Other Countries:*
Contemporary Poets Rewiring History (2014). *Nothing More* (Arc,
2013), which samples the Polish poet Krystyna Miłobędzka, was
shortlisted for the 2015 Popescu European Poetry Translation
Prize.

JAMES WOMACK is a translator from Russian and Spanish. His
selection from Vladimir Mayakovsky *'Vladimir Mayakovsky' And*
Other Poems was published by Carcanet in 2016.

LIDA YUSUPOVA is the author of several other books of poetry
and prose, including her most recent book of poetry, *Dead Dad*
(Kolonna Publications, 2016); the prose collection *Love Has Four*
Hands (Kvir, 2008; co-authored with Margarita Meklina); and
another poetry collection, *Ritual C-4* (Argo-Risk, 2013); as well as
many publications in magazines and journals.

SERHIY ZHADAN is a Ukrainian poet, fiction writer, essayist, and
translator. He has published over two dozen books. The English
translations of Zhadan's work include *Depeche Mode* (Glago-
slav Publications, 2013), *Voroshilovgrad* (Deep Vellum Publishing,
2016) and *Life of Maria and Other Poems* (forthcoming with Yale
University Press in 2017).

KSENIYA ZHELUDOVA, born in 1990 in Leningrad, has published
two collections of poetry, *Slovno* (2013), and *Navernost* (2015). She
works as a multimedia producer and regularly publishes new
work on social media.

JOSEPHINE VON ZITZEWITZ is a scholar and translator
specialising in later Soviet and contemporary Russian poetry.
She is currently teaching at the University of Bristol.